# *Will You Trust Me Even If You Don't Understand Or Can't See What I'm Doing?*

"How To Overcome Negative Emotions &
Difficult Circumstances Through Faith In Christ"

By

**Andrew Bills**

# Will You Trust Me Even If You Don't Understand Or Can't See What I'm Doing?

"How To Overcome Negative Emotions & Difficult
Circumstances Through Faith In Christ"

Copyright @ 2014
All Rights Reserved
Printed in the United States of America

By

**ABM Publications**
A division of Andrew Bills Ministries Inc.
PO Box 6811
Orange, CA   92863

**ISBN:  978-1-931820-41-7**

# *Special Dedication*

To:

## Bishop Napoleon D. Rhodes,
## Bishop Peter E. Hickman
## and
## Bishop John H. Edwards III, Esq.

Thank you for mentoring me,
exemplifying faith, courage & the love of Christ Jesus,
and for believing in my God given dream

### *Forever In My Heart & Prayers*

# Table of Contents

# *Forward*

**"A devotional is a spiritual thought or prayer that helps one gain an insight to who and what God is; It enables one to become more fervent, faithful and dedicated to a particular person or thing. It's one's private reach to the God he serves; It is man reaching Godward." NDR**

As was said of David, Pastor Andrew Bills is truly a man after God's own heart. He labors to please Him in everything he does and believes in excellence, giving his best in every work or task.

His striving to do God's will has led him to help others reach out to God, knowing He is the answer to all of life's challenges. But many find it difficult to break through without being fed; for many are yet babes (1st Corinthians 3:1-2). They see the bottle but can't reach it or they need someone to put it to their mouth. Once done, they will freely drink and be filed.

Pastor Bills has taken the bottle of The Holy Word, mixed the formula in the right proportions so that the milk helps the little ones grow. Having read several of Pastor Bills' daily devotionals, I was very impressed with the beautifully deep yet simplistic presentation of material, which reaches the heart of the reader \hearer and touches his or her soul. His messages answer many questions as to how, why and when God will move in the life of an individual and what happens when an expected answer does come or doesn't come the way one may expect. You can tell from the devotionals that much prayer has gone into the preparation and God has visited the man.

In the 16th Chapter of St. John, the disciples adjure Jesus not to speak to them in parables any more, but to speak plainly to them. Pastor Bills must have heard the disciples' plea for his devotional messages are beautiful and plainly delivered.

### *Bishop Napoleon D. Rhodes*

## 1st Prelate of The Convention of Covenanting Churches

Andrew Bills

# *Acknowledgements*

"What is most needed today in this time of many bewildering troubles is good spiritual teaching. This is what the human heart is really hungering after. But not just any spiritual teaching will do. What is needed is an authentic spiritual teaching that is rooted in the Gospel of Christ and borne by an authentic relationship with the person of Jesus. This is what Pastor Andy Bills gives us in this book.

Practical and applicable teaching that has been tried and proven in the crucible of his own life. His writing is simple and direct but not simplistic. It is pastoral in style and profound in insight.

Pastor Bills displays the pastoral sense of the Apostle Paul as well as the wisdom of Solomon. Therefore I am pleased to commend this work of my friend and colleague, Pastor Andy, to both the beginner and the seasoned follower of Jesus."

### *Bishop Peter Elder Hickman*

### Presiding Bishop of The Ecumenical Catholic Communion

"Pastor Andy's reminders that we must actively seek God through our prayers and actions are a tremendous inspiration to me. Through his messages I am taught that I need to seek my answers from God and His words as recorded in the Bible and live the life in faith that God intends for me."

### *Gay Smith*

### Businesswoman

Andrew Bills

# _Introduction_

## _"Will You Trust Me_
## _Even If You Don't Understand_
## _Or Can't See What I'm Doing?"_

Will you trust God if you're being lead in ways that may seem peculiar or drastically different from the ordinary way of doing things? Will you trust God if His will clashes with your personal plans, wars against your physical desires, conflicts with your natural thinking, defies your human logic and even challenges your existing faith?

This is a series of messages that **NO BELIEVER SHOULD BE WITHOUT!** Not only will you learn **"the hardest spots in life can also become a place of new revelation or a brand new beginning,"** but you'll learn **how to overcome negative emotions and difficult situations through faith in God's Word and experience The Holy Spirit mightily moving in your life.**

Drawn mainly from of the story of Luke Chapter 5, these messages are powerful, insightful and gracious prophetic words that were wonderfully inspired by The Holy Spirit of God. With additional insights from some of the most horrific, painful, challenging & devastating experiences that I've ever encountered, through which Christ has brought me.

**These messages of victory are for those whose lives have been shipwrecked because** of adverse circumstances, hard times, bad financial decisions, ungodly relationships, unforeseen or unexpected events, bad choices, abusive situations, chemical dependencies, painful conditions, loneliness, slander, divided homes, and even past hurtful church experiences.

Just like I discovered, you too should realize that the help you truly need will **NOT** come from moving to another community, finding a new love interest, watching TV talk shows, losing weight, making new friends, finding a new job, winning the lottery, having another drink, smoking another cigarette or even eating another slice of pie. **"<u>NO</u>!"**

**Arising from your wounded past will only come from fully embracing Christ, our Living Savior. Place your confidence in his Word and trusting that by His Grace he will save, deliver, guide, heal, comfort, strengthen and provide for you as you turn to and fully walk in obedience to God.**

Therefore, allow these words to inspire and assist you towards having a joyous fellowship with The Living Christ, which will bring you face to face with divine opportunities from God.

### *THEREFORE, HAVE FAITH IN GOD!*

## "The Victory Report Hour"

### The Internet, Radio & TV
### Global Outreaching Bible Teaching Ministry Of:

**Pastor Andrew Bills**
**Victory Fellowship Church of Orange**
**PO Box 6811**
**Orange, CA 92863**

## www.andrewbills.com

# *Will You Trust Me Even If You Don't Understand Or Can't See What I'm Doing?*

"How To Overcome Negative Emotions & Difficult Circumstances Through Faith In Christ"

# 1

## "Will You Trust Me Even If You Don't Understand Or Can't See What I'm Doing?"

Today, The Holy Spirit would like to ask you a very personal question, **"Will You Trust Me Even If You Don't Understand Or Can't See What I'm Doing?"**

God wants you to realize that if you're going to place your confidence or faith in Christ, many times you'll be directed in ways that will be peculiar or drastically different from the normal way of doing things. His Will may clash with your personal plans, war against your physical desires, conflict with your natural ways of thinking, defy your human logic and even challenge your existing faith.

**Are you aware that, if you obey The Lord, God can do more in one day of your life by His Grace than you could ever accomplish in a whole lifetime of hard labor without Him?**

**In Luke 5: 1-11 NIV** we are given an amazing example of this.... **Luke 5: 1 says,** "One day as Jesus was standing by the Lake of Gennesaret, the people were crowding around him and listening to the Word of God."

The fame of Jesus of Nazareth, as a great teacher, prophet and miracle worker had begun to spread widely. Wherever He went, regardless if it was in the synagogue, marketplace, a desert area or by the seashore, a great multitude of people would quickly gather around Him.

So on this occasion, Luke says the people pressed upon him to hear the Word.

1

**The Word of God, in the hands of The Holy Spirit, is the transforming power of God and is available to everyone today.** People are running everywhere in an attempt to grasp, handle or control their own circumstances and destiny in their own strength. But discouragement, heartache and failure are often the results because there's something special about what God can do that you can't, even if it's in your own life.

When you get into His Word, His Word actually gets into you, becoming one with you and produces a change. The greatest change that you need first begins within you, then around you. I found that out when I gave myself totally over to the Word, that people who could have been viewed as my enemy, God gave me victory over. **I can't control what someone else thinks about me, but I have control of what I think about you and God gives the victory.**

**Verses 2-3 says,** "He saw at the water's edge two boats, left there by the fishermen, who were washing their nets. He got into one of the boats, the one belonging to Simon, and asked him to put out a little from shore. Then he sat down and taught the people from the boat."

The ancient Jewish Historian Josephus says that on an average day there were 230 small fishing boats on the shore, each attended by four or five men. Along with a multitude of people that had come out to see him from throughout the region, lead to an even greater crowd of people pressing in to see and hear Him.

Jesus decides to use Peter's boat as His pulpit from which to preach to the large crowd of people. In the form of an amphitheater, Jesus is elevated on the boat so He could be more visibly seen and heard as He proclaims The Word to all the people.

**Now, I want you to visualize this picture.** Jesus is elevated up above the people so He can proclaim the Word to the crowd. Notice, I said, **"He's elevated upwards."** The Holy Spirit said,

**"Anytime I AM elevated and have your undivided attention, you've positioned yourself for a blessing."** When you elevate Jesus in your life, in your home, over your circumstances, then get ready for supernatural, divine, spectacular and miraculous things to occur. We need to elevate and worship Him constantly in our lives. **Have you given Him first place in your life?**

**Verses 4-5a says,** "When he had finished speaking, he said to Simon, "Put out into deep water, and let down the nets for a catch. Simon answered, "Master, we've worked hard all night and haven't caught anything....."

I want to pause right here for a moment and allow The Holy Spirit again to ask you: **"Will You Trust Me Even If You Don't Understand Or Can't See What I'm Doing?"**

Listen to the anguish in Peter's voice when he said, **"Master, we've worked hard all night and haven't caught anything."** Even overwhelmed from the frustration from an empty catch, while initially wanting to express his doubts, Peter called Jesus, **"Master."**

They were exhausted, discouraged, disillusioned, depressed, cold and empty handed. No doubt as Peter turned about and looked at their naked hooks and empty nets, he wanted to object to what Jesus was directing them to do. It clashed against their thinking: it defied their human logic, and it challenged their present state of being. **For they were expert fishermen.**

Now, if any of you know anything about fishing, you know you go fishing before sunrise, but now it was close to noon. The Lord had given him instructions to launch out into the deep to catch fish. Peter knew this was against any fisherman's wisdom. So, Jesus' instructions or command was contrary to Simon Peter's own human logic.

If you're going to put your confidence and faith in God, many times you'll have to remember that He's going to lead you in ways that may seem to be peculiar or drastically different from the normal way of doing things. His Will may clash with your personal plans, war against your physical desires, conflict with your natural thinking, dare your human logic and even challenge your existing faith. You must prepare for growth by allowing your faith to rise to a higher level as you're confronted with new situations or difficult circumstances.

**Just like Simon Peter, so many people today have restricted God, limiting Him to what they can visually see.** They limit God to what's in their bank account, to their own natural talents, to what they can feel, hear, see, taste or smell but **God's saying,** "I need you to elevate Christ in your life. Place Him first and look to Me. He's again asking, **"Will you trust me even if you don't understand or can't see what I'm doing?"**

My friends, I don't know about you, but I was just like Simon Peter, when he said, **"Master, we've worked hard all night and haven't caught anything."**

Out of anguish, have you ever thought to yourself or said to God, **"Lord I've worked my fingers to the bone, I've done everything I know to do to try to make ends meet, but it's not working. Lord, I've given everything to this marriage and it seems to be on the rocks. Lord, I've given this boss all of my energy and I keep getting passed over for this promotion. Lord, you know that I'm lonely, I've been seeking your face for a mate and I've done everything I know to do."**

The Lord's still asking you, **"Will you trust me even if you don't understand or can't see what I'm doing?**

When we look into the Holy Scriptures, the Bible's full of examples where God blessed people in ways no one could ever have imagined. The Scriptures say that all believers need to **"walk by faith, not by sight."** You've got to look to Him, count on Him and learn to trust Him.

**"Well Pastor, you don't understand. I've been praying for my husband so long and the more I pray for him, the worse**

he gets," declared one woman in my congregation. God knows all about it, but He never gave up on some of us and some of us were worst than some of the ones for whom we are now praying.

God has the ability or power to transform lives, but His hardest problem is not raising the dead or curing the sick. **God's hardest problem is getting you to submit, surrender, commit and then cooperate with Him.** That's what God wants, **"Obedience;"** for obedience is better than sacrifice and **"obedience is the key to the miraculous."**

**In verse 5b Peter continues,** "But because you say so, I will let down the nets."

**At thy word - At thy command, I will go and let down the nets.** Though it doesn't seem rational or it's highly unlikely that they would catch anything after having worked all night in vain, yet he was willing to obey the words of Jesus and venture back out and let down his nets.

This was a remarkable instance of faith for Peter because at this moment he knew very little about Jesus. He was not the chosen apostle he later came to be. Jesus came to these fishermen at the beginning of His ministry almost a stranger. **Yet Jesus' words pierced the heart and captured the mind of Peter and once more they sailed out into the deep.**

**Have the Words of The Lord impacted your heart and soul?** If all would just obey Him and place their trust in God. You will discover that He always backs up all of His promises and never disappoints anyone that calls upon the name of The Lord.

**What is The Lord saying to you out of His Word?** Somewhere in every one of our lives, there's a scripture, there's a Bible verse, there's a story, there's a passage that is applicable to our situation or to whatever our need is that God has spoken.

**There's nothing new under the sun.** The same old devil is attacking us with the same old hashed-up temptations. But God's

Word is fresh and all we have to do is turn to Him and say, **"Yes Lord, I'm going to stand on this promise and I'm going to trust you."**

My friends, He's been given the name above every name, and at the name of Jesus, every knee shall bow and every tongue shall confess that He is Lord. There's strength, salvation, healing and deliverance in His name. I've seen God change the hearts and lives of people that we've prayed for. Some used to be alcoholics but now they're going home taking care of their wives and families. I've seen God miraculously heal dope addicts and give them a love for His Word and the only thing they get high on now is The Holy Spirit. I've seen God heal the sick, and if he doesn't miraculously heal you, he'll give you strength for that hour so you can enjoy that day as you continue on your journey. Thank you, Jesus.

**Verse 6 says,** " When they had done so, they caught such a large number of fish that their nets began to break."

The Lord so wonderfully blessed them that they couldn't even begin to contain the fish that Jesus miraculously brought to them. Obedience to the words of Jesus produced a dramatic change of events in their lives. They caught such a great amount of fish that their nets began to break because of the weight and number of the fish.

The question again is, **"Will you trust me even if you cannot see or you don't understand what I'm doing?"**

Now is the time for you really to believe God. No situation, such as a recession catches God off guard. A recession usually is perpetrated by sinful and greedy men in high places, resulting with many innocent people suffering. But in order for us to succeed in any area economically and socially, we have to turn our hearts to God in order to survive. We can't look to anyone else because everybody else is letting us down. **God has allowed circumstances to bring us to that place where you have to learn to trust Him and praise Him.**

**Verse 7 says,** "So they signaled their partners in the other boat to come and help them, and they came and filled both boats so full that they began to sink."

The God we serve and obey is **"More Than Enough."** One of the promises of God is if your life pleases him, his blessings will overtake you. You don't have to seek after things, just seek Him and walk in obedience, and His blessings will overtake you.

**What blessings?** Does that mean we're all going to get rich? Can we name it and claim it or blab it and grab it? No. I admit; many people are saying, "Lord, I'm believing you for that Cadillac." **But what about your life with Jesus?**

**Do you have a relationship with Him?** "No, but I'm believing God for that new home or new car." No, God doesn't work like that. He's not Santa Claus or The Tooth Fairy!

He's interested in maturing and raising you up. As you surrender and walk with Him, he's going to use your testimony to help someone else who's coming along behind you that you can encourage, strengthen and help guide them towards trusting Jesus Christ. **"Will you trust me, the Lord is saying. Will you trust me?"**

**Verses 8-9 says,** "When Simon Peter saw this, he fell at Jesus' knees and said, "Go away from me, Lord; I am a sinful man!' For he and all his companions were astonished at the catch of fish they had taken."

He fell down at Jesus' knees – Recognizing the power and authority of Jesus; he prostrated himself to the ground, trembling and afraid. Peter and his associates had never experienced anything like this before. Their boats were in danger of sinking because they couldn't even begin to contain the amount of fish that were being caught.

Peter was so convinced that Jesus was a messenger from God that he felt unworthy even to be in his presence. The Lord took this man who declared that he was a sinner and He made him into one of the greatest fishers of men that the world has ever known.

This event so changed the heart of Peter that when **Peter got up off that ground, he no longer thought about the fish or the value that it would bring him from the market.** He only thought about his relationship with Christ. He prioritized his relationship with Jesus to be more important than money.

So many people think that the dollar is almighty. No, God is greater than the American dollar or any other world currency. He's wiser than all the information or knowledge on the Internet. Whatever you need, whatever your situation, whatever your circumstances, He's calling you to enter into His presence and walk with Him.

**Verses 10-11 says,** "and so were James and John, the sons of Zebedee, Simon's partners. Then Jesus said to Simon, "Don't be afraid; from now on you will fish for people. So they pulled their boats up on shore, left everything and followed him."

Jesus calmed their fears and to their surprise He announced that from that moment on they would become fishers of men. They forsook all, their small boats, nets and fishing gear and followed Jesus. It may not have been much, but it was everything that they owned to make their living.

**Do you love Him more than the things that you possess?**

# 2

# "Are You Allowing What You Think Or How You Feel To Hinder You From Trusting God?"

Again, The Holy Spirit would like to ask you this personal question, **"Will You Trust Me Even If You Don't Understand Or Can't See What I'm Doing?"**

If you're going to put your confidence and faith in God, many times you'll have to remember that He's going to lead you in ways that may seem to be peculiar or drastically different from the ordinary way of doing things. His Will may clash with your own plans, war against your physical desires, conflict with your natural thinking, dare your human logic and even challenge your existing faith. You must prepare for growth by allowing your faith to rise to a higher level as you're confronted with new situations or difficult circumstances. Many times people think they're operating in faith when they're actually walking in their own intellect, thereby limiting, restricting, restraining or placing boundaries on The Lord.

**Hebrews 11:6 says,** "Without faith, it's impossible to please Him, for he who comes to God must believe that He is and that He is a rewarder of those that diligently seek Him." If you are to trust Him, you first must believe **"HE IS"** and then that He is a rewarder of those that diligently, sincerely and earnestly seek after Him.

**Have You Made God Your Priority?** Once you've begun to seek His Face then you'll discover the hand of God moving in your life and circumstances.

So God is personally asking you right now, **"Will you trust me even if you don't understand or can't see what I'm doing?**

To help you receive revelation from The Holy Spirit of God, **let's now consider 2 Kings 5: 9-11.** "So Naaman came with his horses and his chariots and stood at the doorway of the house of Elijah, and Elijah sent a messenger to him saying, go wash in the Jordan seven times and your flesh shall be restored unto you and ye shall be clean. But Naaman was furious and went away and said, 'Behold, I thought he would surely come out unto me and stand and call on the name of the Lord his God and wave his hand over the place and cure the leper.'"

The story of Naaman may be a familiar story, but it's filled with many important kingdom principles of faith. As The Holy Spirit personalizes this story to your heart, once again He's asking, **"Will you trust me even if you don't understand or can't see what I'm doing?"**

Now Naaman wasn't just a soldier, he was the General of the Syrian or the Aramean Army, second in command to the King. Naaman was a man of great power and was held in high esteem throughout his country and by his peers. He had conducted many exploits from which he returned back victorious. He had slaves; he had wealth and a notable name. He had everything going for him, but at the beginning of this chapter, it lets us know that he had one battle that he couldn't conquer – **"Leprosy."** Somehow he had contracted this dreaded skin disease that was now threatening to destroy his promising future.

How many times have you considered your upcoming future and made certain plans when all of a sudden something wrong happened? An unexpected accident or tragedy, an unforeseen major sickness or an unanticipated job layoff, then suddenly your hopes, plans and dreams are shattered, and life begins to take a downward spiral.

Back in those ancient times when a person contracted leprosy, they were immediately excluded from society and forced to live in remote valleys or desolate caves in a far away desert area. They would be fed by those who would literally throw food off the cliffs or lower it in baskets, and this was their plight until they died.

**Leprosy, believed to be incurable, led to a deplorable lifestyle that Naaman never expected.** This disease left him weak, broken in spirit and would soon leave him deformed, disfigured and disgraced. As he looked back on all of his successes and victories, this was not what he had envisioned, and none of his great accomplishments could protect him from the fate of this loathsome disease. No doubt a man of his stature may have even called on all the doctors, wizards, soothsayers, enchanters and witches with their remedies that were around, but to no avail.

After all of his efforts had been exhausted, in his household there was a little female slave who was from the nation Israel that waited upon Naaman's wife, that finally spoke up. Even though she was a slave, she testified of the miraculous power of the God of Israel and said in verse 3, **"I wish that my master were with the prophet who is in Samaria! Then he would cure him of his leprosy."** Her witness was so convincing that Naaman believed and decided to go there.

So Naaman gathered his large entourage full of chariots, soldiers, horsemen and his entire staff. He took many expensive gifts, silver, gold and many costly garments, and he went into Israel in search of his healing. Eventually, he was directed to the house of the Prophet Elisha and arrived with great pomp and circumstance.

Upon arrival, Naaman sent someone to the front door to summon the prophet to come out. Elisha, who knew that he was coming, didn't even bother to go out and greet Naaman, but just sent out instructions for him to **"Go down to the River Jordan and just dip seven times and he shall be clean."**

Elisha didn't refuse to meet Naaman face to face because he was a leper. No, Naaman was so full of pride and overestimated himself and this was God's manner of humbling him.

Naaman was an important man and not used to being treated with such disrespect, so he became furious. According to verse 11, because of his notoriety, Naaman thought that the prophet would at least come out and honor him, stand before him, then call on the name of The God of Israel, wave his magic wand, perform some mystical or spectacular event, or call down fire from above. Naaman honestly believed that Elisha would do something supernatural, dramatic and exciting because of who he was and the distance that he'd traveled. Yes, Naaman was so full of pride that he even presumed how the God of Israel should heal him by the prophet's hand. **But what does The Lord say about pride?**

**Proverbs 16:18 NIV says,** "Pride goes before destruction, a haughty spirit before a fall." **Then Proverbs 6: 16 -19 NIV says,** "There are six things the LORD hates, seven that are detestable to him: a proud look, a lying tongue, hands that shed innocent blood, a heart that devises wicked schemes, feet that are quick to rush into evil, a false witness who pours out lies and a person who stirs up conflict in the community."

**Are you aware that God doesn't work the way a person feels or thinks He needs to work?** No, my friend, The Holy Spirit is saying to you again, **"Will you trust me even if you don't understand or can't see what I'm doing?**

**God is not going to do His will your way.** So often people try to tell God how to do things, when it should happen and by what means it should occur. God does not perform miracles or send blessings the way you want them to happen. Often when you believe God to move in a particular way, He comes in an entirely different manner. The God we serve, when he stretches forth his hand, does it to get the glory and give you a greater testimony so you can bear witness only to Him.

Often the Word of God may appear contrary to our human wisdom but God's looking for obedience and obedience is the key to the miraculous. God's a mind-blowing God who doesn't always come at the exact moment when you want Him, the way you expect him and He doesn't show up and move the way you think He should.

**Isaiah 55:8 says,** "God's thoughts are above our thoughts, His ways are above our ways." We see things from our own viewpoint or level and begin to develop our plans from where we sit. But when God gets ready to bless and move in your midst, He intervenes supernaturally by His Spirit and through His Word, in a way so that you'll thoroughly understand that your victory or breakthrough only came as a result of His Grace.

My friends, Christ today can yet turn your mess into your special message and make sense out of the nonsense you're experiencing. Again, The Holy Spirit is asking, **"Will you trust me even if you don't understand or can't see what I'm doing?"**

Naaman was so upset, furious and angry that he began to spew fire as he began to cry out in verse 12, **"Are not Abana and Pharpar rivers of Damascus, better than all the waters of Israel? May I not wash in them and be clean? So he turned and went away in a rage."** While he turned to go home, it's important to note that Naaman would not have been healed if he washed in another river. While there wasn't anything special about the water in the Jordan River, it was God's command and going to another river would have been complete disobedience.

Even if God's will seems foolish, **"Will you trust His Word?"** So often if people don't get or can't see the immediate results they desire, they want to give up. They want to surrender or throw in the towel, but that's the time to stand and trust God. **Do you believe Him? Are you standing on His Word?**

Standing is an act of aggression. When you stand, you are attacking back by placing your confidence in The Lord and worshiping Him. When you worship God, you are acknowledging in the middle of your adverse circumstances that He's the lifter of your head and not the breaker of your back.

**"Will you trust me if you don't understand or can't see what I'm doing?"**

**The staff of Naaman came to him and they said,** "Look, master, if he'd asked you to do something spectacular, something out of the ordinary, would you have done it?" They tried to pacify or calm him down and finally they brought him to a place that he could hear the words of the prophet again. Naaman humbled himself, swallowed his pride, accepted the advice of his staff and obeyed the words from the Prophet Elisha.

So he made his way to the River Jordan, then in his costly attire and in front of his entire entourage; he walked directly into the muddy, cold, rigid overflowing waters of the river. Then he dunked himself one time, a second, third; and each time no doubt when he came up, he looked at his hands to see if there was any difference. So he proceeded and kept counting. He dunked a fourth, fifth, sixth and still there was no difference. Finally, he dunked a seventh time. **Let's read what the Scripture has to say in 2 Kings 5:14,** "So he went down and dipped himself seven times in the Jordan according to the Word of the man of God and his flesh was restored like the flesh of a little child, and he was clean."

On that seventh time when he went down, he came up and there wasn't a gradual change, no he came up and immediately his skin was cleansed, soft, pure, and as clean as that of a newborn baby. I can envision Naaman shouting in that water. You might say, **"Well Pastor Bills, the Scripture doesn't say that."** I know it doesn't, but I know what I would have done if I was Naaman and I know what I've done every time when God has mightily moved in my life. It became a time of shouting, rejoicing, thanksgiving and wonderful praise. So Naaman was overwhelmed, blessed, might have cried, might have shouted, might have even splashed water up all over the place, but he was never the same again.

**How do you know that?** Because Naaman publicly declared in verse 15, **"That there is no God in all the world except in**

**Israel."** Then after he left that river, he went back to the prophet's house and met him face to face and tried to be a blessing onto him.

Naaman learned that the goodness and grace of God can't ever be bought with silver and gold or manipulated by the power, position or prestige of a man. **All must come to The Lord in faith by trusting Him and His Word.**

Now, there were many other lepers around, both Jews and Gentiles, but only Naaman ventured forward to seek out the prophet for a cure from God.

Again, The Holy Spirit is saying, **"Will you trust me even if you don't understand or can't see what I'm doing?"**

When we call on God to move in our lives, we are to take our burdens to the Lord and leave them there. Leaving them there means you get up, and you go about your business believing that God has heard and is now working things out for His glory and your best. **You don't pick up the burdens and carry them back away.** Leave them there, even if you don't see anything positive, supernatural or miraculous occurring. Stand in faith on God's Word and continue to look to Him.

**"So, Will You Trust Me Even If You Don't Understand Or Can't See What I'm Doing?"**

# 3

# What Should You Do If God's Will Doesn't Make Any Sense To You?

Are you struggling with the call of God or wrestling with the will of God in your life?

Again, I want to remind you that if you're going to put your confidence and faith in God, many times He's going to lead you in ways that might seem to be peculiar or drastically different. His Will may clash with your physical desires, conflict with your natural thinking, dare your human logic and even challenge your existing faith.

**When God calls you, no man or woman is fully qualified. He calls you to do something that you cannot do alone.** Jesus gets the glory by working through you; you get the testimony of being used and along the way you and the people surrounding you become impacted by the grace and power of God.

**For Isaiah 55:8 says,** "God's thoughts are above our thoughts, His ways are above our ways." We see things from our own viewpoint or level and begin to develop our plans from where we sit. But when God gets ready to bless and move in your midst, He intervenes supernaturally by His Spirit and through His Word in a way so that you'll completely know that your victory or breakthrough only came as a result of His Grace.

If it challenges you, remember that God will supply the anointing, power, resources and the people to effectively do the work that He's called you to do.

**So we need to learn to go and flow with God.** When His will begins to clash, contradict, go against or go in another direction from where you want to go, you must learn to stop and obey Him and follow His direction.

As you walk in faith and obedience to God's Word, supernatural signs, visions, dreams, prophetic words or spiritual encounters will be used by The Lord to confirm, assist to direct or encourage you as The Holy Spirit of God wills.

When you do this, you'll learn that you'll have a greater outcome, and He'll get the glory.

**Let's consider the calling and leadership of Gideon in the book of Judges, Chapters 6 and 7 to help bring insight to your heart regarding this.**

With the passing of the previous generation in Israel under Deborah and Barak, forty years of devotion, peace and prosperity were now gone and long forgotten.

The Lord looked down on Israel and once again they had fallen into sin and turned away from The Lord. With a new generation now on the scene, **"the Israelites did evil in the eyes of the Lord."** By refusing to obey God, He allowed the enemy to rise against them.

**Judges 6: 1-11 describes in great detail the deplorable conditions that Israel had been reduced to.** God allowed the Midianites to afflict, oppose and enslave Israel. They were unmerciful nomads that invaded the land to ravage it. They plundered the land, stole the livestock, caused great destruction and made life unbearable for the nation of Israel. In order for the Israelites to survive, they fled and hid in mountain clefts, caves and strongholds and there they began to call on the name of The Lord. So God began to go to work on the heart of a man who would become Israel's answer to prayer and next deliverer.

The Angel of The Lord came and personally appeared to Gideon, who was hiding and trying to cover up what he was doing in a winepress. **Judges 6:12 NIV says,** "When the angel of the LORD appeared to Gideon, he said, "The LORD is with you, mighty warrior."

Now from every natural standpoint, Gideon did not appear to be a deliverer, a judge, a strong man of any quality to lead Israel into victory. It was quite the contrary. Gideon was a weak man, full of doubt and fear, living in a pagan home, which had ceased looking to God and was now filled with idolatry. But God came into his situation and began to move in his life, calling him by name and then referring to him as **"mighty warrior."** God saw potential in him that he couldn't see in himself.

While Gideon's response began to imply reasons why he felt that he wasn't suited for this leadership role, The Angel of The Lord told him that he was because, **"I will be with you."** God's presence is more than enough and makes all the difference in any task, position, or work than we are called to do.

Gideon was full of doubt, skepticism, and fear, so he didn't understand the direction from The Lord. **So, wrestling with uncertainty, Gideon asked for a sign as proof to substantiate this calling and The Lord condescended to his request.**

**"Does Asking God For A Sign Imply A Lack Of Faith?"**

**Is asking for a sign or confirmation evidence of doubt or disbelief in a person's heart?** It appears that Gideon's requests, in Judges Chapters 6 & 7, for signs weren't because God responded to them and according to **Hebrews 11:6,** God never responses to unbelief.

Furthermore, it seems that after all the supernatural signs and evidence from God, Gideon finally realized the supremacy of the one that had been speaking to him and it strengthened his heart.

While the Bible has many different historical accounts of miraculous signs, when a person's heart revealed that they were earnest, God chose to use them to reveal Himself and His Will in different ways.

**When a person's heart was wrong, demanding a sign was always refused by our Lord because of their wickedness.**

Now while signs are not essential, God requires us to trust Him without any outward or physical evidence other than placing faith in His Word. **But whenever The Lord deems it necessary**

**to use signs as a means of validation or encouragement, He will do what's necessary to make an impact upon the heart and mind of that individual.**

Now it's important also to know that not all signs are from The Lord. Just as Pharaoh's magicians were able to duplicate some of the miracles of Moses in **Exodus 7: 20-22,** some workers of iniquity are able to produce counterfeit signs today. **Many have been known to try; create and manipulate signs to prove their anointing or suit their own selfish wishes.**

So believers must study God's Word, learn to depend upon The Holy Spirit of God for the gift of discerning of spirits, see if it glorifies The Lord Jesus Christ and remain steadfast in the faith.

**We must learn and remember that signs are only used to confirm God's Word and His Will in our lives. We are only to be led or guided by The Holy Spirit, who uses God's Word as light to direct our pathway and footsteps.**

Signs are only a gift of God's grace as He deems necessary but they lack the power to transform the human heart. Only God's Word, being used by The Holy Spirit can do that.

**So instead of pursuing signs, seek Christ Jesus.** Whatever dream, vision or supernatural evidence that He thinks you might need to assist you, will come only as The Holy Spirit wills.

**So devote yourself to The Word of God, get in God's presence, listen to The Holy Spirit and in all your ways acknowledge Him, and He shall direct your path.**

Finally, this fearful, weak and cowardly man, now called and empowered by God, began to recruit and rallied a 32,000 manned army. But even with these limited capabilities, Gideon asked for more signs and again God answered His request.

Gideon had successfully gathered together 32,000 men to stand up against an opposing army of 135,000 soldiers. While they were still greatly outnumbered, untrained and lacked military weapons, he thought that he might still have a chance, but God began to speak, informing him that he had too many.

**"What should you do if God's will doesn't make any sense to you?"**

God gave two tests that would eventually reduce Gideon's army of 32,000 men to a soul staggering 300.

First, The Lord instructed Gideon to speak and tell them, **"All the ones that are afraid and all the ones that are trembling to go back home."** Truly Gideon had to think that it didn't make any sense to him and that no one would leave. But to his surprise, 22,000 men (two thirds of his small military) quickly dropped their weapons and departed for their homes. This had to be a shocking experience to Gideon.

God then told Gideon that the reason he was sending them home was that even with his small army, if they got the victory they would boast of themselves and not give Him the glory. The Holy Spirit is saying that the battles that you are facing, the victory that you are believing him for will not come by your power, or your might but by My Spirit, saith The Lord. **(Zechariah 4:6)**

Though the way he's leading and directing you might clash with your human understanding, you need to learn how to flow and go with God. Though the hand of God may move differently from how you expect or even desire, God will share His glory with no one.

Now I know if you were Gideon you would be saying, "If you went to battle with the 32,00 men, you would still make sure that God would get the glory" but God looks into the heart of men. So God said, **"tell them to go home."** Again to his amazement, 22,000 departed. **But God was still there and in control. Sometimes it's important to remember that when God is all you have, HE'S TRULY ALL THAT YOU NEED.**

Finally, God gave the second test which resulted in Gideon's army being reduced by another 10,000, leaving him with just a mere 300 men. But God assured Gideon that his band of 300 men were more than adequate, with His help, to defeat the Midianite coalition army.

The way God moves is contrary to human reasoning. Sometimes we think we can acquire the victory because of our strength, our power, our intellect, our natural talents, the money we have in the bank or our personal connections. But God looks into our hearts and sees what we can't see. If we learn to flow and go with God, we'll be saved, healed, delivered, and receive the victory over all of our circumstances.

Even though God knew that Gideon was still nervous and afraid to attack, still referred to him as a mighty warrior or a man of great valor. Before Gideon could ask for another sign, God commissioned Gideon to **"get up and go down against the camp because I am going to give it into your hands."** (Judges 7:9)

Obediently, he crept into the enemy camp and overheard one of the soldiers telling another about his dream of destruction from Gideon's army. (Judges 7:13-14)

While the Lord had previously revealed a victory to Gideon seven times earlier, hearing these words from the mouth of the enemy was a great turning point in Gideon's character and leadership.

**What were the natural chances of this taking place?** God had directed his steps so he could be in the right place at the right time to hear these words.

When you allow God to direct your path, even if it doesn't make sense, God will lead you to your victory. If his directions clash with your human reasoning; you must surrender, submit, commit your will and go with God in order to experience victory.

With secrecy, planning, suddenness, simplicity and perfect timing, Gideon's men were armed only with trumpets and lamps hidden in jars. Quietly, they came upon the Midianite camp and blew their trumpets and smashed the jars and shouted their battle cry, **"The sword for the Lord and for Gideon!"**

Broken lights and mass confusion brought destruction to the sleeping Midianites, who believed they were under attack by a larger army of soldiers. Under the cover of darkness, many turned on one another with their swords while others fled into the night, only to be pursued and later destroyed.

Like goodness and mercy, signs and wonders will always follow those that believe. As you walk by faith, God will bestow many different acts of grace, signs or prophetic words to encourage you on your way.

**THEREFORE, HAVE FAITH IN GOD!**

# 4

# "How Dependent On God Are You?"

To shed more light on the power of His words and to help believers understand the connection of Himself to His Church, Christ presented the relationship of what the vine is to the branches.

**In John 15: 5 NIV Jesus said,** "I am the vine; you are the branches; he who abides in Me and I in him, he bears much fruit, for apart from Me you can do nothing."

The connection, association or union between the vine and the branch is **"A LIVING ONE."** It is the union between the human soul and our divine Lord and Savior. He is the True Vine and we are His branches.

The branch is born, develops and continues to derive its life from the vine's sap that flows into it and gives it energy to blossom and yield fruit. **The life of the branch is solely based upon its attachment to the true and living vine.** For if it lives, the branches will also live. But without the vine, the branches are unable to stand and sustain life.

The Lord used this parable or metaphor not just to teach but to invite us and encourage us to **"Live In Him."** So intimate is the connection between the vine and the branch that without it, the branch is nothing.

The life of God through Jesus Christ is through the **"Living Sap"** or The Holy Spirit. It's through Him that we live, move and have our being. It's through Him that we are given the power to live the Christian life, bring forth fruit and have the anointing to render service for the Lord. We are totally dependent on Him, **"For without Him, we too can do nothing!"**

Just like the roots of the tree are unseen, our life is hidden in Christ Jesus. The roots cause the tree to grow and then sends the sap up through it, ultimately giving its life and strength to the branches.

**All that the vine then possesses belongs to the branches. Jesus, in His prayer before God, said in John 17:22,** "The glory which You gave Me, I have given them."

Then the branch outwardly demonstrates the excellence of the vine by the fruit that it yields. The branch only has one reason to exist or one purpose for living:  **to blossom and produce.**

God, who is **"The Husbandman or The Vine-dresser,"** is so watchful over His Vineyard that His Church can't help but flourish and prosper even in this dark and evil world. The forces of darkness have tried and failed in every attempt to afflict, wreck, crush, pollute, infiltrate, stop and try to destroy The Church of Jesus Christ, all without success because The Church is built upon a solid foundation with Christ as its corner stone.

Jesus Christ is the True Vine, who will continue to nourish us, supply us, restore us and empower us to bring forth fruit abundantly.

**As a branch of Jesus, are you resting in Him, waiting for Him, serving Him and living so that He may demonstrate and reveal the riches of His glory and grace before a dying world?**

# 5

# "Did You Know That God Wants You To Face Your Circumstances In His Miracle Working Power?"

God wants you to learn how to face all of your circumstances in the strength and power of His Word and Holy Spirit. God invites you to swim and not sink or drown. He's calling you to stand and climb, not to stumble and fall. God is maturing a people who will do just that in the face of all adversity: to stand on His Word, stand for Him, and face every trial, test or crisis victoriously in The Name of Jesus and in The Power of The Holy Ghost.

**In the 27th chapter of the Book of Acts,** The Apostle Paul was a prisoner on board a ship that was sailing for Rome. Just prior to leaving the harbor, he warned the captain that he sensed in his spirit that their voyage would not only be damaging to the ship, but very dangerous and even life threatening to all those on board.

**But Paul's words were not believed!** And the orders were given, and the captain set sail for the open seas. Shortly thereafter, there arose a very severe typhoon or hurricane, which lasted several days. During this time they experienced one of the most heart wrenching ordeals, the likes of which the 276 soldiers, crew members and prisoners had never before experienced.

Their ship was being threatened, in danger of being torn apart and sinking. For many days they saw neither the sun nor the moon. So to lighten the ship, they began to cast all their tackle and cargo overboard. Terror and fear struck most of their hearts and eventually there was talk among the soldiers of mutiny and of killing all of the prisoners, and no doubt suicide may have even entered into some of their minds. But during the very midst of all their struggles, Paul spoke out firmly and boldly in faith.

**Acts 27:22 records the words of The Apostle Paul.** "Be encouraged, for there shall be **NO LOSS** of any man's life among you, only of the ship."

What boldness, what authority, what confidence! Or what nerve! Was he crazy or was he operating under the power and the Grace of God? How or with what source could he back up his bold statement?

**Then in verses 23-24 Paul claimed his source, that he had received a vision of an angel of The Lord who had appeared unto him saying,** "Fear not Paul, thou must be brought before Caesar and, lo God has given thee ALL THEM that sail with thee."

Then Paul firmly, boldly and publicly declared, **"I BELIEVE GOD** that it shall be even as it was told unto me." **But would he be believed?** Would the others trust his revelation from God? How reliable was this in their minds? **Who's Report Would You Have Believed?**

Can't you see the devil at work saying, "Well, why doesn't God just stop the storm? Look things haven't changed! If God loved you or cared, He wouldn't let you be going through all of this. You're never going to make it out of this! You're getting what you deserve. You're all going to die! There's no way out of this hopeless situation!"

These are just a few of the demonic suggestions that Satan implants into the human mind whenever faith is trying to take a stand and express itself in God.

Fear, doubt and unbelief are the three mostly used **"tools of distraction"** that he uses to affect your thinking and control your actions as he tempts you into depending on your senses to shut out all the areas of faith.

Then in verse 31, Paul observed that the soldiers were planning to jump overboard, **so he said to the captain,** "Except these abide in the ship, ye cannot be saved!"

Paul stood firmly and boldly upon the revelation and the Word from God. He chose to believe in the power and the grace of the invisible God rather than the events of the storm. And they finally believed and obeyed his words.

*NOW PLEASE LISTEN VERY CAREFULLY!* The typhoon or hurricane was still very real. The waves of the raging sea which were still coming into the ship were still very real. The food shortage was still very real. The earlier talk of mutiny and murder had been very real. The threat of the ship sinking with everybody on board and drowning in the sea was still very real. Not being able to distinguish night from day for over 14 days was very, very real. The quicksand and the rocks were still a very real threat. The violent blowing wind and the intense rains had not ceased. In other words, the complete physical or outer circumstances **DID NOT CHANGE!**

**But something different was now taking place.** They were all depending on, trusting in and believing the words spoken by The Apostle Paul from God. And through faith, they were emerging from the very face of destruction and was about to learn one of the most important lessons in life, **THAT THE STORMS OF LIFE DO NOT MOVE THE HAND OF GOD.... "ONLY FAITH DOES!"**

God, through His Word, by His Spirit, out of His Grace and by His Direction was **"now making the difference."** For God, who is **More Real,** Jesus Christ, who is **More Real,** and The Holy Spirit, who is **More Real** than the crisis, entered into Paul's circumstances and began to orchestrate everything simply because Paul chose to stand and focus on God's Word regardless of what he was facing.

One man's faith in God brought deliverance to everyone on board. One man's faith led to all 276 souls being saved from destruction and death. All because they chose to listen and obey the instructions and stayed on board until Paul gave the signal to leave the sinking ship.

After the ship was finally driven upon the rocks of a nearby island, they all cast themselves overboard following the instructions of The Apostle Paul, **WHO WAS STILL A PRISONER.**

As they cast themselves into the sea, they even assisted one another, crew members, soldiers and prisoners. They all safely made it to the shore. And just as God's Word had earlier been revealed and spoken to Paul, "Not one soul was lost!"

**NOW WHAT SHOULD THIS MEAN TO YOU TODAY?** It means that your answers to prayer, your deliverance, your healing, your blessings, or your victories are **NOT** based upon the appearance of the physical, or the natural circumstances or on them being immediately changed! Therefore, **STAY ON BOARD IN FAITH!**

Does God Always Keep His Word? **"YES HE DOES!"** Faith in Christ will always make a difference in our lives. God may not always promise you "a calm passage," but He Does Always Promise You "A Safe Landing."

When your marriage experiences bumps in the road, **STAY ON BOARD!** When your financial picture doesn't look so good, **STAY ON BOARD!** When your body is experiencing sickness and pain, **STAY ONBOARD!** When you're facing opposition, and you're not sure just what to do, **STAY ON BOARD!** Stand on God's Word in faith. Stand in faith; looking to Jesus Christ and trust in Him.

Now, I can't help but wonder what impact this entire event made upon the remaining years of the lives of the rest of all those men. But, I do believe that after this they all had an entirely different concept and appreciation of God. Stop and think what can be done when you stand up and step forward trusting The Lord Jesus Christ.

Remember that as you stand facing your challenges and struggles, you too will see that **GOD'S MORE REAL AND MUCH GREATER THAN ANYTHING YOU COULD EVER EXPERIENCE.** Everything's subject to the Word of God and the moving of The Holy Spirit of God.

*AGAIN, LISTEN VERY CAREFULLY!* Often God's Divine Intervention is not one singular movement or act. **IT'S AN UNFOLDING!** It's a revealing of one piece of the puzzle at a time. And it's always to be continued, with the next puzzle piece or the unfolding of the next page of the map yet to be revealed. **BUT YOU MUST STAY IN FAITH TO GET THERE!**

God's Divine Intervention! How amazing, how loving, how powerful, how glorious and how wonderful Jesus Christ is to us that believe on Him.

Spiritual revelations and supernatural manifestations from God come into our daily lives to help us as we're dealing with all the different events we're facing. Certain challenges and situations that cannot be successfully dealt with or overcome by any reasonable means or methods **CAN BE HANDLED BY THE LORD.**

God Always Responds To Faith In The Heart Of A Believer....

**THEREFORE, HAVE FAITH IN GOD!**

# 6

## "Has The Lord Ever Given You A Stone Instead Of Bread?"

Have you ever earnestly prayed for something and later greatly regretted that you got it? **There are both biblical and modern-day examples in which God eventually granted the persistent yet stubborn and imprudent prayers of his people of which they later lamented or mourned over, repented from, or were very sorry about.**

If hindsight has taught you anything, you should be anxious for nothing and be careful what you're repeatedly asking from The Lord . Sometimes God grants to people what they cry out for foolishly, selfishly, lustfully, and sinfully, consistently want.

Such was the case of Israel as they began, however, to repeatedly cry out to God for a king. **Then in 1 Samuel 8:9 NASB, God gave The Prophet Samuel the following information and instructions,** "Now then, listen to their voice; however, you shall solemnly warn them and tell them of the procedure of the king who will reign over them."

**Israel wanted to be like the other nations and relentlessly pressed in on The Prophet Samuel to make God give them a king.** They wanted the pomp & circumstance, the splendor of the marching army with proud colors, and the parades that the other countries exhibited.

Their pursuit demonstrated their ingratitude towards The Lord that had brought them to where they were, and now they believed they were more capable of directing their own affairs from there.

So a tall, humble, handsome, intelligent looking and strong young man named Saul was chosen to be their new king. But as the years passed and history records, he became evil, hateful, jealous, deceitful, enraged, greedy, and deranged, as he continually disobeyed and turned his back on God. **God gave them exactly the type of king they asked for, but later they totally regretted that decision.**

**Have You Ever Prayed For Bread And Received A Stone Instead?** I've personally counseled women whose hearts have been crushed from marrying men they requested from God. They believed that they could change them into a more perfect husband. Time revealed that these women experienced bigger demons.

There have been some men who believed that a certain business venture or career change was God's best for them only to encounter a satanic entrapment, financial ruin, and years of painful stress as they've later attempted to rebuild their lives.

Many couples have invested their financial savings into the hands of an investor only later to discover that he was unscrupulous, a wolf in sheep's clothing, and robbed them of their hard-earned savings.

If you've made any mistakes in any of these areas, **then learn that while experience has become a teacher, you don't have to let it become your undertaker.** Ask The Lord for forgiveness and allow His Word to renew you and His Holy Spirit to heal, restore, rebuild, and lead you onward.

**We may not actually know what is the best for us, so be careful what you repeatedly ask of God. Don't become over anxious or too quick to jump into anything.** Make sure you're listening to and following the leading of The Holy Spirit of God. It's no harm to seek some godly advice from a spirit-filled pastor or even ask other Christians to pray with you before making certain decisions or choices.

31

It's no harm at all even to ask God for a **"spiritual confirmation"** before making some life-changing major decisions. **Another useful piece of information is to step back away from it for a brief period and get before The Lord in fasting and prayer, then take another look and see what God is saying to your heart.**

Make sure it's in His best interest because He really is concerned about you. **Your welfare means so much to The Lord that He gave His life upon the cross because He always had your best interests in His Eternal Plan.**

# 7

# "Are You Aware That God Has Special Plans For You?"

If you're a believer, God has made you a joint heir through Jesus Christ and has special plans for you. **For you've been called out of darkness, set free and filled with His Spirit with the potential to fulfill His Will.**

It's not in the mentality of God for you to think that you've been saved just to go to heaven when you die and just sit around idle until then. **You've been called into fellowship with God and to experience the power of His Spirit living through you to make changes in your home, community, church, city, country, and even the world by standing up in faith through Jesus Christ.**

Now, Satan will lie and try to make you think that you're a failure, that you can't amount to anything. You're useless, that you lack the courage, that you're situation is hopeless and that you don't have what it takes to be used by The Lord. He will tell you that you're not saved, anointed enough, or have not been saved long enough to do His Will, **but that's a lie from the pit.**

**For God chooses and uses ordinary people, just like yourself, to be a witness and example before the world regarding the power of God through Jesus Christ.** He enables you to serve Him and He's the one you are to look to for your guidance, wisdom, and strength. **You must learn and remember that wherever the Will of God will take you, The Grace of God will keep you.**

**In 1ˢᵗ Corinthians 1: 26-29 NLT, The Holy Spirit said through The Apostle Paul,** "Remember, dear brothers and sisters, that few of you were wise in the world's eyes or powerful or wealthy when God called you. Instead, God chose things the world considers foolish in order to shame those who think they are wise. And he chose things that are powerless to shame those who are powerful. God chose things despised by the world, things counted as nothing at all, and used them to bring to nothing what the world considers important. As a result, no one can ever boast in the presence of God."

Gideon was afraid, Moses complained that he couldn't speak well and Barak the general refused to take his army to battle unless Deborah the Prophetess accompanied him. Samuel was just a child when called by God; the Pharisees called Peter and John ignorant and uneducated fishermen and just like them, the world often taunts us Christians as **"losers."**

**But our victory and success is not dependent just upon our human knowledge, physical might, natural talent, or earthly resources.** God has always shown His power by choosing and using the under-qualified, the abandoned, the weak, the obscure and the unlearned. Those that God uses are those who will humble themselves, be pardoned by His grace, stand on His Word and be filled with His Spirit in or to be mightily used of Him.

Christ has even used young children and teenagers that are led by Him to silence the mouths of some elite infidels and those that believe they are in the highest ranks of humanity.

**The flesh of proud men always stands in opposition to The Spirit of God and the opinions of the world are in contradiction to the divine wisdom and the anointing that comes from above.**

By bestowing His Grace on the humble, The Lord has a lengthy history of confounding the wise to bring to them to shame, **just to reveal to them how little their wisdom contributes to the success of His Divine cause.**

God has redeemed you and wants to elevate you through His Word and the power of His Holy Spirit to do things that the world cannot understand or resist.

**Will you surrender, submit, and commit yourself to Jesus Christ and His Will for your life?**

# 8

## "Standing Up Through
The Storms In Life Through
Faith In God"

Years ago I received an emergency call from a family in my church and immediately left my job as I rushed to the hospital. **The pregnant wife's family was being informed that due to her sudden severe illness, the possibility of her carrying a baby to full term was in jeopardy, and even if the infant did survive, the child would be born with severe retardation.** So, they were recommending terminating the pregnancy.

As their pastor, I was allowed into the intensive care ward and quickly taken to her room. She had been sedated and was being given other needed medications as she was being cared for. So I quietly stood along her bedside and began to call upon **THE GREAT PHYSICIAN, The Lord Jesus Christ.**

I already knew Him as a doctor, but could I believe that He wouldn't lose this case? As I sensed His Presence, I realized Christ never cares about your previous medical history, doesn't look at medical charts, doesn't care about the diagnosis, isn't concerned how you got to this place, and doesn't even review your X-rays. I had long discovered that when things even appear hopeless, **There's Always His Grace, so I prayed.**

As I prayed, I tenderly held her hand. Then knowing her heart, even while she slept from the medication, I entered into an agreement before God to believe Him for the birth of a healthy baby and the healing of this mother and her life. I took authority over the condition, the sickness, and the circumstances, all in the mighty name of Jesus Christ. **I fully believed and confessed that when Jesus hung on that cross, He died that she and her**

**baby would live.** I quoted scriptures over her and I prayed with such fervency until my clothes were drenched with perspiration.

**I firmly stood on John 15:7 where Jesus Christ said,** "If you abide in me and my words abide in you, then you shall ask what you will and it shall be done unto you."

Any believer in Christ who has engrafted God's Word into their heart, realizing their union or relationship with Christ, charged with His thoughts, burning with His purposes, allowing His Words to control or affect their lives, will have no will that is not in harmony with the Divine Will of God.

**I prayed according to God's promises in His Holy Word and stood in faith that not only would He do what He said He would do in His Word, but that it was already done through the death and resurrection of Jesus Christ.** Then after embracing and encouraging her family, I went home.

This family had a major decision now to make. Would they believe in The Lord that I represented and that a few of them had come to know personally? **Would they believe in the words and encouragement of their pastor from the Holy Bible?**

As a young pastor, I had come to know the extreme importance of knowing Christ, believing in The Power of God through prayer, and the importance of giving good biblical and spiritual counseling as I looked to the Lord.

That Sunday morning I preached, telling the church that **"often God expects us to believe Him and His Word without any outward sign or evidence apart from faith in the name of our Lord and Savior Jesus Christ."** No matter how dark, dismal, or discouraging our situation may seem to be, we are instructed and encouraged to have faith in God. **Everything is predicated on what God has already done for us through Jesus Christ.** The Lord wants us to believe and have faith in Him despite our surroundings and what they dictate to us. We are to be open to the voice of The Holy Spirit of God for further direction.

That family stood in faith. They believed in a God that I had taught them about, and they looked to Jesus Christ. **Several weeks later, that mother gave birth to a very healthy strong baby boy, and over the years I watched him grow throughout childhood.**

That mother didn't know that I had come into her room and prayed like I did. While she was later told of my visitation and prayer, I jokingly teased her that I had to buy a new suit because I never had prayed before where my suit had become so drenched that it couldn't even be cleaned. **We all laughed as we were filled with great joy and gave God the glory.**

As a further result of this, the majority of her family came to church. Some members of her family came who had never darkened the doorway of a church before in their lives. Many came to Christ and began reading the Bible for the first time.

There's Nothing Too Hard For God To Do, but the issue at stake is, **"Will You Trust Him And Believe In His Word?"**

# 9

# "Where Do You Go From Here?"

Sometimes as you go through life, **you may have to begin a brand new chapter in your journal by starting again.** Initially you may also be filled with questions, anxieties, or uncertainties after being overwhelmed by the things that have happened around you. **But then you'll have to learn how to proceed from that place of unhappiness or devastation.**

This may occur after experiencing the death of a loved one, after a divorce, a job layoff, the foreclosure of a cherished home full of precious memories, after being faced with a long-ranged road of recovery from an unforeseen sickness, an abusive situation, or addiction of chemical dependency.

It may even come after a heart-wrenching decision to depart from a church you've been in for years and not being clear as to where you're going next.

While God doesn't promise immediately to unravel or resolve every one of our problems, He does instruct, encourage, and expect us to place our full confidence in Him, for He says in His Word that **"The Just Shall Live By Faith."** (Habakkuk 2:4)

The Prophet Habakkuk became perplexed and began to wonder, complain, and ask God questions regarding the things that were happening during his day. Just like many today, he wanted to know: **"Why are the wicked prospering? Why is God allowing such horrific and sinful crimes? Why does it seem as if God is silent during these evil times? And why is God destroying the less evil nation of Judah by permitting a much more wicked nation, like Babylon, to conquer them?"**

Finally, in the very midst of all the confusion and difficulties, Habakkuk went up to the watchtower to get alone with God.

There, after praying, he learned to listen to God and hear His answers. It was there that God revealed to him His ultimate plan for His people.

**When a nation turns its face from God, its rebellion or sin will be judged.** So God revealed to the prophet that He was going to use Babylon to afflict Judah, but Babylon's turn would then come and be blotted out. **But God, in His infinite wisdom and love, would remember His people and give to those that repented and sought His face a more glorious future.**

The inspiration, insight, and revelation that Habakkuk received from The Lord was so great that he began to shout a special song of praise and put his total trust in God, despite what was yet occurring around him. **(Read Habakkuk 3:17-19)**

He realized that **"today"** is just a small part of God's eternal plan and **"All things work together for good to them that love God, to them who are the called according to His Purpose."** (Romans 8:28)

You too must come to realize that in the midst of every tribulation and the darkness of every storm filled with misery, it's through faith in Christ and standing firm on God's promises that we will find ourselves being sustained, comforted, and strengthened by His Holy Spirit. So, know that whatever you're going through today, **THIS TOO SHALL PASS!!!**

Whenever you're tossed, perplexed, and being overwhelmed by the events around you, remember God's precious promises to you that are in His Word. **Our hope is anchored in Christ.**

Observe, adhere to, and obey the answers given in His Word that are anointed and made alive through The Holy Spirit of God. **Then will you hear what Christ has to say to you in every situation.**

**Habakkuk learned and prophesied that those who wait to hear His Voice will not be disappointed. Though the answer may seem as if it's being deferred, it will come and be made abundantly clear as you wait on The Lord.**

Just like a shipwrecked survivor will cling to a life preserver, we too must hold fast to God's Living Promises, for He alone is Our Salvation, Security, Protector, and Deliverer. Neither Christ nor His Word is confined, limited, or powerless to hard times, adverse circumstances, negative situations, painful conditions, or the demonic activity that surrounds us.

**Then at the very end of our road, we shall find our great eternal reward through our Lord and Savior, Jesus Christ.**

# 10

# "Did You Know That God Wants To Take You From Where You Are To Where You Need To Be?"

God wants to broaden your horizons and take you from the **"old and familiar"** to a brand new level, **but have you become so comfortable that you don't want to move and go forward?** What's holding you back today?

**The Holy Spirit declared through The Apostle Paul in Romans 12: 2 NASB,** "Do not be conformed to this world, but be transformed by the renewing of your mind, so that you may prove what the will of God is, that which is good and acceptable and perfect."

One of the greatest enemies of believers today is conformity to this world. It's you being overwhelmed with minding earthly things that instead of renewing your mind in God's Word and walking in the Spirit, you're operating in the flesh and not being effective for Christ.

I've met many believers who can tell you the complete history and current statistics of the many different athletes, **but they can't quote any scriptures or share Christ with anyone.** Then let the truth be told that "Normal Christian Living is considered **abnormal** by many of the folks that claim to be believers or by folks who just go to church somewhere."

The word **"Mind"** is used 95 times in The Holy Bible, which simply means a place of consciousness, perception, understanding, feeling, judging, reasoning, determining, and choosing. **It's the place where our thoughts are born, reside, and then become action.** From that point our character is forged, shaped, and outwardly manifested.

Once a sinner has been saved by Christ Jesus, it's here that God wants to impact, renew, and fill you with His Word that you might not sin against Him, grow in faith, and learn to walk in the power of The Holy Spirit of God.

The mind is the heart, soul, and center of your personality, decision making, and your every action. Again, it is here that Christ wants to influence, but this responsibility is now yours because **faith comes by hearing and is developed, nurtured, and then becomes stronger through the consistent renewing of your mind in His Word.**

The work of The Holy Spirit first begins in the understanding, then His Word affects the will, affections, conversation, and actions until there is a change of the whole being into the image of Christ in knowledge, righteousness, and holiness. **One cannot live godly unless there is a giving up of one's self to Christ Jesus.**

There's no other way for this to happen. There are no shortcuts that you can take. Reading, studying, and meditating in His Word is you spending time in His Presence, receiving inspiration directly from Him.

Through disciplined reading, studying, meditating, and praying in the Holy Scriptures, several things will begin to happen within and around you. **You'll begin to erase Satan's false and negative programming of your fleshly mind, thereby crushing the devil's control ability over you and your surroundings.**

Through the ongoing studying of The Bible, you'll increase your ability to obey God. **Obedience is your key to the intimate, supernatural, divine, and miraculous hand of God moving in your life and orchestrating in your affairs.**

It's through the studying of God's Word that you'll see yourself being set free from all past guilt and condemnation. **Then you'll also be able to eliminate the success and effectiveness of their demonic attacks, entrapment and deception.**

Through the renewing of your mind in God's Word, you'll receive guidance and direction for your life and walk in the anointing of The Holy Spirit of God. **There's just so much more to the heavenly riches that are in Christ Jesus to all that will follow Him.**

Many desire and want these things, **but are you willing to deny yourself, pick up your cross, and follow Jesus?**

# 11

## "Do You Really Believe In The Power Behind The Cross Of Jesus?"

On July 1, 1824, Charles Finney, an ordained Presbyterian minister, appeared in a number of churches and other buildings to lead revivals over the next few decades throughout New York and Pennsylvania.

Preaching three times on Sundays and three more times during the week throughout the **"red light district"** in these states, **great revivals broke out. Finney taught that the atoning blood of Jesus Christ was all that was needed to open up the way for God to pardon people of their sin.** Only by repentance and the acceptance of Christ in one's soul could one be saved from damnation and Hell's fires and be assured of a place in Heaven.

**A great decrease of the criminal activity in these areas was solely attributed to his gospel preaching and leading of thousands of sinners to Christ.**

On one particular occasion, as Finney was about to enter the church he was to preach at, a man approached him and asked if he could privately speak with him after the service. Finney said yes, and after entering the building, a deacon pulled him quickly to the side and said, **"Do you know who that man is?"**

Finney said no. The deacon said, **"Don't have anything to do with him. It's rumored that he's the one responsible for all the gambling, drugs, prostitution, and murders in this city. He's a really bad man! Don't have anything to do with him!"** Finney said that he had given his word to meet him after the service and must keep his word to see what he wanted, and he entered the church.

After the service, that man was waiting for Finney on the doorsteps of the building. Finney greeted him and the man said, **"I would like to speak privately with you. Can you come to my office?"** Finney said yes and began following him.

They walked a couple of blocks and then suddenly turned down a dark alley before coming to a door that led downwards into a small room in the cellar. In the room were just an old desk and one chair.

As the man sat down, looking up at Finney he said, **"Do you know who I am?"** And Finney responded, **"Yes."** Then the man slowly reached into his desk drawer and pulled out a gun and laid it on top of the desk and said, **"I'd like to ask you a question."**

He proceeded, **"It has been said that I'm the one responsible for all the gambling, drugs, prostitution, and crime in this city. Can God forgive a man for having done all of these things?"** Finney replied, **"In First John 1:9 it says, if we confess our sins, he is faithful and just to forgive us *our* sins, and to cleanse us from all unrighteousness."**

The man just nodded and then said, **"There are several families that have been ruined because I've had their husbands or fathers murdered. Can God forgive a man for having done all of these things?"** Finney again responded, **"In First John 1:9 it says, if we confess our sins, he is faithful and just to forgive us *our* sins, and to cleanse us from all unrighteousness."** Again, the man just slightly nodded his head.

Then the man said, **"I'm married and have a little daughter that I rarely see because I've been with several other women. Can God forgive a man for all of this?"** Once again Finney declared, **"In First John 1:9 it says, if we confess our sins, he is faithful and just to forgive us *our* sins, and to cleanse us from all unrighteousness."**

Finally, the man just looking up from his desk at Finney in the dimly lit room said, **"You can now go."** And without another spoken word from either, Finney departed.

After sunrise the next morning, the man went home. Upon hearing the front door unlock, the man's wife quickly told her daughter that **"Your daddy's home but whatever you do, stay out of his way."** The man entered his home.

Upon smelling the scent of the breakfast, he entered into the kitchen where they were nervously standing. He walked over to his little daughter and picked her up and held her for the first time in his arms and kissed her cheek and told her how much he loved her. Then he proceeded to embrace his wife, and after kissing her, he asked her forgiveness for all that he'd ever done to her and announced that their lives would never be the same again because of Christ.

You don't get to Heaven by being **"good"** or go to **Hell for being "bad."** The Bible says we're ALL born in sin or all bad, and we've ALL fallen short of the Glory of God and in need of a savior. God, therefore, saves those who believe in His Son, that He died on the cross for them and washed their sins away. **Then God not only forgives our sin, but also purifies our heart.**

The Eternal Son put on flesh and blood and died to wash us from our sins in his own atoning blood that we may have a new relationship and intimate fellowship with Christ and be destined for Heaven.

**God Himself has provided the sufficient and effectual Sacrifice for sin that is needed throughout all the generations of mankind, without which a person is lost forever.**

# 12

# "Are You Allowing Fear To Hold You Hostage?"

The Black Panthers, a radical militant group of the 1960's and 70's, began to threaten the City of New York. They declared that they would start blowing up all the bridges through the city unless their demands were met. The authorities responded by imposing curfews, conducting roadblocks and massive manhunts, scouring the city for them without any initial success.

The leaders of the FBI appealed to a very prominent Black Pastor, Dr. E.V. Hills in Watts, California, to speak to the black community throughout the country to help stop the threats of this siege. When Dr. Hill met with J. Edgar Hoover, he asked, **"How many are involved in that radical movement?"** Hoover replied, **"There are 89 militants involved."** Dr. Hill responded, **"89 people are holding two million people hostage in New York City? How is that possible?"**

**Fear had brought the city into being held captive, not the 89 militants.** They were being held hostage in their minds, and fear was producing unlimited possibilities of mischief and destruction in their thoughts.

**When fear holds you hostage, it will appear to be more powerful, soul-shaking and life threatening than your ability to try to deal rationally with it or spiritually overcome it.**

**2 Timothy 1:7 says,** "For God hath not given us the spirit of fear, but of power, and of love and of a sound mind."

God has not given us the spirit of fear, but the spirit of love, power, and courage to face any difficulty and overcome all danger. **Through The Holy Spirit, we will be strengthened** and enabled to confront and go through all opposition with a sound mind which is guarded by the peace of God, that defies all understanding.

**Being fearful is a matter of choice.** You may not be able to choose what will happen to you in life, but you clearly can choose the attitude you'll take in responding to things that happen. **You will either choose to be fearful or stand in faith, believing God for His assistance.**

The Apostle Paul exhorted Timothy to hold fast, to stand strong upon, and to trust the Holy Scriptures. **In doing so, you too will come to realize the unspeakable value of The Word of God and experience the divine and gracious intervention of Christ in your midst.** For God hath not given us the spirit of fear or a cowardly spirit, to be afraid of sinful wicked men or evil demonic forces. We must not be distracted or detoured from living our lives, doing God's will, preaching the Gospel, speaking out against false teachers, reproving people for their evil deeds, and touching the world with the love of Christ.

**Fear is a tormenting spirit that bombards your mind, creates mental anguish, and wants you to surrender control over to others.** It causes people to become frightened, stressed-out, and even paranoid. But God wants you to stand strong against this spirit, resist Satan's temptations, to endure hardness as a good soldier, and be victorious over **"the spirit of quitting."**

Through Christ, you've been given the power to stand up under all the various trials and be triumphant under persecutions. **Though your faith might be tried with fire, we are kept by the power of God through the shed blood of our Lord and should know that the love of Christ Jesus will enable the weak to be strong and stand up in a world that's fallen down.**

Christ has given us His Holy Spirit with many precious promises in His Word. Without Him, we can do nothing, but with and in Him, there's nothing that we cannot do.

**THEREFORE, HAVE FAITH IN GOD!**

# 13

# "How Can I Let Go When My World Is Being Turned Upside Down?"

This was the question that I was frantically asked by a believer that was being overwhelmed by her circumstances.

**The main reason that people are troubled is because of trying to figure it all out alone.** Once you stop trying to orchestrate or manipulate the outcome of things, cease from striving for your own solution, and stop blaming others for your past mistakes or failures, then you can hear God speak. Then you can **"BE STILL"** before Him, hear from The Holy Spirit, and learn to yield to God's plan.

Now, as painful or difficult as some situations may seem, God's now calling you to **"BE STILL"** and stand in faith before His Presence.

**Psalms 46: 1-2 says,** "God is our refuge and strength, a very present help in trouble. Therefore we will not fear, though the earth be changed, and though the mountains slip into the midst of the sea."

**Then in Psalms 46:10 God says,** "Be still and know that I AM God, I will be exalted among the nations, I will be exalted in the earth."

These are just two of the many different passages of scripture that should be able to give you unshakable confidence in knowing that God will always protect and provide for His children. But the secret in learning to trust God to be your **"refuge, strength, and help"** only comes from learning how to **"be still"** before The Lord.

"Well, how do you do this when I'm having a financial crisis or have suffered the loss of a loved one or have just experienced a job layoff or a son is arrested for drug possession or my unwed daughter runs away because she's pregnant? How can I be still when my husband's having an affair or my wife files for divorce or my dreams have been shattered and I'm even disillusioned with God because my prayers have not been answered?"

**"BEING STILL"** before the Lord doesn't mean that you become physically inactive. It means you are **"becoming open to The Lord"** in order to hear His Voice and be led by His Spirit. It means you are becoming more attentive and ready to obey and follow His directions and His Word. **"How can you hear from God when your mind is filled with confusion and just running wild?"** There are certain things God now wants to reveal to your heart and mind, but you can't hear or receive from Him while you're always on the run and being driven by panic and fear.

**In Exodus 14:13-14,** when the Israelites saw Pharaoh and his army coming to destroy them on the shores of the Red Sea, under heart-wrenching circumstances, Moses said, "Fear not, **STAND STILL** and see the salvation of the Lord, that He will show to you today. For the Egyptians whom you have seen today, you shall see them again no more forever. For The Lord shall fight for you and you shall hold your peace." And we all know the great miracle that took place on that day.

**It takes courage and faith for you to surrender and become still.** But, it's a matter of choice. Either you'll choose to worry and remain frustrated, or you'll choose to **"Be Still"** before The Lord.

The devil wants you distracted, disturbed, disillusioned, and defeated. **But Christ is now calling you to get alone with Him.** You can learn to steal away from everything around you and know that your life and your welfare are now at stake. So begin by establishing some time away from the TV and other activities and get before God in His Word. **Learn that if you seek His face, you'll get His hand moving in your midst.**

Despite having worked a full-time very stressful managerial job with more than enough responsibilities and duties, I was totally refreshed and amazed after rising earlier just to spend some quality time with Christ before beginning my day. **It clearly made a difference in my life and circumstances, allowing me to receive inspiration and direction from The Lord.**

Christ will reveal Himself to you as your savior, deliverer, helper, healer, provider, and whatever else you need. No matter what you're facing or going through, God is available, willing, sufficient, all loving, all powerful, full of mercy, and wonderful grace.

HE IS **"your place to run to"** when your world turns upside down and is filled with chaos. HE IS **"your rest and comfort"** when you feel you can't go on any further. HE IS **"your energy and strength"** when you're too exhausted to continue and fight.

**BE STILL AND HAVE FAITH IN GOD!**

# 14

## "Are You Ready To Go To A Higher Level In Your Faith?"

**The Lord wants to take you to "another level in faith," but are you ready to go?** Many of us are just like Martha in John Chapter 11. When she heard that Jesus was coming, she ran out to meet him. Martha loved Jesus, had faith in him, and she trusted him. **But her life had been shattered, her heart torn, and her spirit crushed because of the pain and grief she was experiencing** as the result of the death of her brother Lazarus.

Regardless of what she was feeling or going through, **Christ came to take her to another level in her faith.** He walked into their situation to do something and to reveal something that they had never before encountered. She, just like many of us today, don't fully recognize just how **AWESOME** our Lord truly is. We've limited or restricted Him to what we only can comprehend. But He wants to take your faith to an entirely new level in Him.

Jesus, who was more aware of the distressing circumstances than Martha and Mary knew, came, and upon engaging Martha in a brief conversation to enlarge her expectations and take her faith to another level, declared Himself to be the Resurrection and the Life. **Are you believing and trusting Christ regardless of what you're physically seeing or experiencing?**

At first when Jesus told her that her brother would rise again, she was thinking about the end-time general resurrection from the dead. Christ knew exactly where her thinking and heart were, but **He entered into her situation to draw her out, broaden her expectation, elevate her faith, and heighten her understanding** by demonstrating His Authority, Power, and Grace over all the circumstance regarding man.

**In John 11: 25-26 NASB Jesus uttered these most inspiring words,** "I am the resurrection and the life; he who believes in Me will live even if he dies, and everyone who lives and believes in Me will never die." **Do you believe this?"**

The Lord knows what you're experiencing at this very moment. He's more aware of your adverse circumstance; negative situation, hard time, and painful condition than you will ever know. But despite the dictates of your intellectual mind, emotional condition, natural thoughts, or even Satanic suggestions, **He's come in the power of His Living Word and Holy Spirit to take your faith to another level by trusting Him despite all the things that you see surrounding you.**

**Are you open to Jesus Christ as The Resurrection, your true and only source, the main substance, the first fruits, your redeemer, and our everything?**

Our greatest comfort can **ONLY** be found in Christ Jesus, in His Eternal Words, and in the power of His Holy Spirit. Today **HE STILL IS "THE GREAT I AM"** and forever will be. Will you trust Him even if you don't understand or can't see what He's doing in your very midst?

**Ephesians 3:20 NLT reminds us** "God is able, through his mighty power at work within us, to accomplish infinitely more than we might ask or think."

**THEREFORE, HAVE FAITH IN GOD!**

# 15

## "Are You Following The Yellow Brick Road?"

Are you seeking answers and direction to the situations that you're facing?

In 1939, a motion picture was made that would have a great impact upon our world called **"The Wizard of Oz."** While it's a treasured classic to untold millions, its underlying message is of greater value as Dorothy spends the entire movie just trying to get back home.

Initially Dorothy had run away from home, but an unforeseen tornado resulted in her going to a foreign land. Once there, Dorothy thought she had been brought to a place in which she felt ill-prepared, but all she lacked in her life was **DIRECTION**.

Maybe you're seeking a fresh start, a new beginning, or a dramatic change in your immediate circumstances. Maybe you're seeking for new employment or business opportunity, a new community environment to reside in, or even a new relationship. But you don't have to run away or try to escape to make changes in your life or circumstances. **All you need is "DIRECTION."**

All you need is to seek God's face, walk in His Word, and then you'll experience His Divine Intervention, Grace, and the leading of His Holy Spirit.

God can and wants to provide direction in your life to develop you from where you are. But, you're going to have to learn to lean on and trust The Lord. **Remember, if you want to get to the Promised Land, you first must learn to follow Him.** As you start to follow Him, you'll begin taking the first steps towards recovery or having a brand new beginning.

**Proverbs 3: 5 & 6 says,** "Trust in The Lord with all thine heart and lean not unto thine own understanding. In all thy ways acknowledge him and he shall direct thy paths."

When Dorothy landed in Oz, she was given the wonderful instructions to **"Follow the Yellow Brick Road"** and was advised never to detour from it. Then along the way she made some new friends of great diversity, but she also encountered some new enemies.

As we journey through life, we'll also meet people of different personalities, skin tones, cultural backgrounds, hair textures, intellectual differences, style preferences, and theological variances. **But by trusting Christ, you'll learn how to distinguish those** who will become friends that will help or encourage you from those that are predators sent into your midst to lead you astray, discourage, defeat, or try to destroy you.

God wants to guide you on your journey and do wonderful and amazing things in and through your life. **The pathway for you is always forward in faith from wherever you are.** Your walk of faith will not be a quick sprint or a magic carpet ride, but a life-long journey of obedience, fellowship, and trusting in The Lord. And as you do those things, He Will bring you safely home.

**THEREFORE, HAVE FAITH IN GOD!**

# 16

## "Faith Will Open Your Eyes To New Opportunities If You're Willing To Believe God"

So often people feel sorry for themselves because they only see their negative situation, weaknesses, inabilities, past failures, or where they find themselves in life. **But placing faith in God will change your perspective and affect your outcome.**

Even when God is all that you have, **FAITH will allow you to envision what others cannot or will not see.** Faith sees the possible in the impossible, finds hope in a hopeless situation, and believes that there's nothing too hard for God to do in your life. **Faith says that you are here for a purpose** and that your present difficulties or challenges are nothing more than stepping stones through which you must see new opportunities.

**Faith inspires you onward with confidence that's rooted in the solid foundation of Christ Jesus.** Then faith stabilizes you, holding you rock steady, with the confidence that you can make it as you proceed through the storms of life.

**As God has promised that He will never leave us or forsake us,** FAITH believes that the circumstances you're dealing are not mistakes, but **"springboard"** into new doors of opportunities for growth and blessings as you stand fast on God's word. **Such became the life of a little girl born in poverty and sickness that became a great champion in the world.**

**"Did You Know That triumph can't be had without the struggle?"** declared Wilma Rudolph, whose life was a story of a person achieving against the odds through faith in God.

The 20th of 22 children in an extremely poor black family, she was born prematurely on June 23, 1940, in Clarksville, Tennessee, weighing only 4 1/2 pounds at birth.

Because of racial segregation in the South, she was not allowed medical treatment at a local hospital. So she spent the majority of her childhood in bed with her mother spending those several years nursing Wilma through one illness after another: measles, mumps, scarlet fever, chicken pox, double pneumonia, and then polio.

When her mother was told that Wilma had polio, a crippling disease that had no cure at that time, **they were told that she would never walk.** Her mother then drove to a black medical hospital 50 miles away twice a week until she was able to walk with the aid of metal leg braces when she was only 6 years old.

The doctors taught Mrs. Rudolph how to do the physical therapy exercises at home, so her brothers and sisters took turns massaging her crippled legs every day. Finally by age 12, she could walk normally without the crutches, braces, or corrective shoes. **Not only did she decide to become an athlete, but she soon became a budding basketball star.**

With her first accomplishments to stay alive and get well behind her, her years of treatment with a determination to be a **"normal kid"** finally started to pay off.

Wilma Rudolph was a sight to behold. At 5-foot-11 and 130 pounds, she was lightning fast. She had natural, unexplained ability, saying, **"I don't know why I run so fast, I just run."**

**At the 1960 Rome Olympics,** Rudolph became **"the fastest woman in the world"** and the first American woman to win three gold medals in one Olympics, winning the 100-meter dash, the 200-meter dash, and the 400-meter relay team race.

Despite a poor baton pass, Wilma, the anchor on that relay team, caught up from meters behind and overtook Germany's famous anchor runner. The Americans, all women from Tennessee

State, took the gold in 44.5 seconds after setting a world record of 44.4 seconds in the semifinals.

**This achievement led her to become one of the most celebrated female athletes of all time.** In addition, her celebrity caused gender barriers to be broken in previously all-male track and field events.

It was stated by her coach that **"She did more for her country than what the United States could have paid her for."** In her soft-spoken, gracious manner, she promoted her country and paved the way for more African-American athletes, both men and women, who came along later.

**In 1963** she was selected to represent the U. S. State Department as a Goodwill Ambassador at the Games of Friendship in Dakar, Senegal. **Later that year she was invited by Dr. Billy Graham to join the Baptist Christian Athletes in Japan.**

Before she died in Nashville, Tennessee, on November 12, 1994, of brain cancer, in **1973** she was voted into the Black Athletes Hall of Fame. In **1974** she was voted into the National Track and Field Hall of Fame, then later NBC made a movie about her life from her autobiography simply called **"Wilma."**

**So, remember the wonderful words from 1<sup>st</sup> Corinthians 2:9,** "That Eye hath not seen, nor ear heard, neither has entered into the heart of man, the things which God hath prepared for them that love him."

**THEREFORE, HAVE FAITH IN GOD!**

# 17

## "How Can I Keep Negative Words From Hurting Or Controlling Me?"

**"Sticks and stones may break my bones but words will never hurt me,"** was a children's rhyme I used to sing in my early youth. Little did I know back then how harsh negative criticism and hurtful words could do more damage than objects thrown at me ever could.

**In Proverbs 15:4 God reveals** "The tongue that brings healing is a tree of life, but a deceitful tongue crushes the spirit."

Destructive voices fill our entire world and in time you are bound to meet all sorts of people that will say things that will cause you pain, **for nothing brings hurt or stirs up anger like grievous words from the lips of insensitive or foolish people.** Often it's not from strangers that will affect you most but from negative and hurtful comments from those that you love or care about.

Like an armchair quarterback who has never picked up a football or a backseat driver who can't control the steering wheel of an automobile, those negative voices are always on the prowl in an attempt to instruct, correct, or slander you without ever knowing what it's like to walk in your shoes.

**So why do you care about what others say to the place? Why are you allowing their remarks to ruin your day and hold you back from doing the things you really want to do?**

**Their taunting hurts because you keep replaying their comments over and over again in your head, allowing it to become forged in your spirit.**

By keeping your mind renewed and controlling your thought life you can prevent their hurtful words from having an impact within you by you doing things differently. **By trusting Christ and walking in fellowship with God's Holy Spirit,** you have been given the authority to prevent things from taking control or casting you down. You can be victorious in crushing the works of the devil over your life. While I cannot keep foolish people from making negative or criticizing comments, **with God's help and strength**, I can control my own attitude in how I will react or how I will be affected by what has been foolishly said to me.

**Aren't you aware that you have been given the power to replace bad thoughts with faith-filled, positive, loving and optimistic thoughts?** Surround yourself with people whose lives are full of faith and have a heart for God. **Don't try to argue back with a fool.** Clear up the negativity inside of you and realize how much God really loves you. Become inspired by listening to some anointed gospel music and encouraged through some anointed and life changing gospel teaching. **Learn God's viewpoint by studying His Holy Scriptures.** Learn to respond productively and remain poised and in control whenever you're confronted with rebellious acting or screwed up people.

**Take back that power and fully commit yourself to The Holy Spirit of God. Remember, no one can control you unless you allow their control to reign in your life.** Stop being a victim and learn to demonstrate God's love through your life, in spite of them.

**Are you aware that God had your best interest in view when He sent Jesus to the cross?** So, confess out loudly that you've been redeemed by His blood, forgiven of your sins, filled with His Spirit and are now walking in His Word. **And that God's viewpoint is the only one that matters and that He is the only one you're concerned about pleasing.**

**THEREFORE, HAVE FAITH IN GOD!**

# 18

## "Are You Really Trusting In The Lord?"

A story was reported about a group of passengers on an airplane that suddenly entered an area of severe turbulence. **The passengers were terrified; some screamed while others were visibly shaken.**

Then one of the badly shaken passengers noticed a little girl, sitting very contently as she continued playing with her toys and looking at her books. She clearly showed no sign of fear. When asked why she wasn't afraid during the terrible turbulence she simply replied, **"Because my daddy is the pilot and he's in full control."**

**Well, in Isaiah 41:10 NIV God Says,** "Fear not, for I am with you, do not be dismayed, for I am your God. I will strengthen you and help you, and I will uphold you with my righteous right hand."

While this promise from our Lord was initially addressed to the exiled Jews during their long and painful captivity in Babylon, **it's also addressed to His people today who are going through any adverse, negative and painful circumstances or conditions.**

God made it clear before, and Is once again making it very plain, **"Fear Not, For I AM With Thee."** HE IS the sole reason that we shouldn't ever be fearful. **Romans 8:31 says,** "If God be for us, who can be against us?" What higher consolation can you ever desire or have than the assurance of Him being our Heavenly Father and protector, counselor, and guide to us during times of great confusion and difficulty.

There is no higher honor in life than to enter into His family and be permitted to call the Creator and The Most High God **"Our Father",** and have the Lord of the universe as our Eternal Friend.

**"Be not dismayed"** means that whenever a state of alarm or danger comes, those that trust and look to Him can be calm because of our peace within and our faith in His Words.

We are then given the reason we shouldn't be afraid, **"For I AM Your God."** Our Heavenly Father has declared "I am able to preserve, strengthen, keep and bless you." The God of Heaven is our God and is our source and power, and that power has been pledged for the protection of all that come to Him.

**Furthermore God said,** "I will uphold you with the right hand of my righteousness." **Our Heavenly Father has also declared ,** "I will enable you to bear all your trials with my faithful right hand." We can rely on Our Lord and the power of His Might.

There is no greater security than believing and knowing that you're safe in the hands of The Almighty and Living God.

**THEREFORE, HAVE FAITH IN GOD!**

# 19

# "What Is The Greatest Proof Of The Reality Of God?"

Was it the discovery of Noah's Ark or the discovery of the Dead Sea Scrolls? Is it the continual rising of the sun over the horizon every beautiful morning, the synchronized orbiting of all the planets and stars throughout our universe or the majestic display of the waterfalls in some of our beautiful forests or parks?

No, it's all of the lives that have been and are being **"TRANSFORMED"** by The Love, Power and The Grace of God.

When we were dead in our sins, doing our own thing, unworthy of divine notice, He made a provision for our salvation. We who had no time for Him or no love to return to Him were **"TRANSFORMED,"** infused with the life of His Son, made a partaker of His Divine Nature and now have insight and favor with God. We now live and reign with Christ and are joint-heirs with Him.

Christ's resurrection from the grave is our resurrection from our sins unto spiritual life in God.

This **TRANSFORMATION** is a special work of God in the human heart of man and cannot be obtained any other way, except through Christ. We were **"quickened or made alive"** when our spirit was brought to life. Now our inner nature and character have been changed from death unto life.

**Ephesians 2: 4-5 NIV says,** "Because of his great love for us, God, who is rich in mercy, made us alive with Christ even when we were dead in transgressions. It is by grace you have been saved."

**Through the love of the unchangeable and sovereign God, and the transforming living power of Jesus Christ,** trouble makers have become peacemakers. Abusers have been made responsible people. Racists are now building bridges wonderfully touching lives in other cultures Drug addicts that have been delivered are teaching others about Christ and making them aware of these demonic elements.

**More people are picking up the Word of God to study and hear God's Holy Spirit that used to be involved in all other types of sinful activities, with some even being the promoters of such.**

Criminals have surrendered their lives of crime and are now preaching the gospel of Jesus Christ, men are becoming more responsible in the parenting responsibilities and many others are seeking God's face for their welfare.

Wherever there have been a natural catastrophe, The Church and many other Christian led organizations or agencies are some of the first on the scene to come to the aid of the hurting and suffering.

**Please listen very carefully....** When a person is dead in their sins, there is no life in their soul. It's like looking upon a corpse from which life has departed. There's nothing left but the ruins of that deceased person.

When a sinner becomes **"TRANSFORMED,"** he or she becomes a living soul as their spirit is born-again or made alive. We are then delivered from sin, pardoned, reconciled and justified by God's Grace through faith in Jesus Christ.

While we believers never become **"perfect"** people, those that have been **"TRANSFORMED"** do not go out, practice or live in habitual sin because your whole new desire is to live a life that pleases God.

These things are not bought to pass by anything that is done by you, it is the **"free gift of God"** as we are quickened by His Power.

The saving, forgiving, delivering, healing and transforming power of God is greatest and the most awesome power that you can ever know. So remember, while salvation is free, **IT CERTAINLY DIDN'T COME CHEAP!**

**JESUS PAID IT ALL, WITH HIS BLOOD!**

# 20

## "Has Your Get Up And Go, Got Up And Left?"

**Often God requires that you trust Him without any outward or visible advance sign from Him.** Blessings only come from the heart of God as you trust in The Lord with all your heart and don't lean on your own understanding of things. By putting God first, He promises to guide and direct your path because everything God does **"hinges on F A I T H."**

**Therefore, it's important to understand that God will not bless what you are not willing to do.** Just having good intentions isn't faith, but taking the initiative and going forward is.

**Taking the initiative will always have productive or better results.** Initiative can be defined as one having the energy, drive, vitality, spunk, zip, life, or the spirit to get up and go forward to accomplish a goal.

Regardless if the initiative is spurred on out of the need for survival or if the motivation is derived from an inward desire to achieve, **being assertive, aggressive, and stepping out in faith with perseverance will lead to better results over just sitting around where you are.**

**In 2nd Kings Chapter 7,** we are given the brief dramatic story of four lepers who lived just outside the entry gate of the city of Samaria. Their city was under siege by their enemy and was preventing aid from coming in.

Famine, poverty, sickness, fear, disease, and depression had now taken over the city of God's people. While they were not permitted to mingle with the regular citizens, by living outside the city gates, these four lepers had hoped to obtain daily scraps of relief from those within. But now due to the severity of the famine, they too were about to die from starvation.

**2nd Kings 7:3 NLT says** "There were four leprous men at the entrance of the gate and they said one to another, "Why should we sit here waiting to die?"

**So by faith, they made their decision to arise and fearlessly walked directly towards the camp of the Syrians in hope of finding grace, but not knowing what to expect.**

To their great surprise, they found the enemy camp totally deserted with not a man to be seen or heard. It was later discovered that the attacking enemy abruptly fled in the darkness when The Lord had apparently and miraculously amplified the sound of the four lepers coming which they believed to be a greater attacking army with horses and chariots. **So, seized with great terror, they quickly fled, leaving all of their cattle, tents, money, garments, food, and other resources behind as thousands of them ran off into the pitch darkness of night.**

So the lepers having discovered all of the riches left behind, instead of trying to keep it all for themselves, decided to report the good news to the officials and people in Samaria, which immediately ended their severe famine.

**These four lepers would have died if they had continued to sit around waiting for some supernatural sign to appear telling them to get up and go.**

God blesses what you do, not what you sit around and just think about doing. **Just having good intentions won't get you anywhere. You must learn to make decisions and then move forward in faith.** It's not enough to just pray for a job. You must arise, go fill out applications, send out résumés , make telephone calls, and go on interviews if you want to work.

**Laziness and indecisiveness are lethal to succeeding or obtaining the victory.** You cannot continue to wait for things just to happen to you. **Never let it be said that your get-up-and-go has got-up-and-left.**

Fear, doubt, unbelief, or solely depending upon your own ability to **"reason or sort things out"** is a mistake. Sometimes your greatest hindrance is **"Yourself."** Take the initiative, make the effort, remain prayerful, take the step of faith, and believe God to make things happen in your home, business, life, and church.

**Then you too will experience the dynamics of The Holy Spirit as you stand on God's Word and step out in faith, in the mighty name of The Lord Jesus Christ.**

**THEREFORE, HAVE FAITH IN GOD!**

# 21

# "Are You Believing Your Doubts Or Are You Doubting Your Beliefs?"

**Faith in God enables us to do whatever The Lord has placed on our hearts to do.** Jesus openly declared that all difficulties, trials, negative circumstances, hindrances, or obstacles could be overcome, removed, dealt with, or conquered through **FAITH in God.**

**In the gospel of Mark Chapter 9: 14-29**, we're given the story of Christ coming down from the mountain after experiencing a mighty transfiguration before 3 of His disciples and walking into a confusing scene. A father had brought his son, who was completely being controlled and tormented by demonic spirits, to the other 9 disciples to cast them out and bring healing to the son, but they could not prevail in their endeavors.

The father, then observing the Lord returning, went running and pleading to Him for the healing and deliverance of his son. After describing some of the deplorable demonic activities, he asks Jesus to help them.

**In Mark 9: 23 NIV it says,** "'If you can'?" said Jesus, "Everything is possible for one who believes." **Then the man's desperate, tearful, heart-wrenching, and agonizing response in Mark 9:24 NIV was,** "I do believe; help me overcome my unbelief!"

Out of sheer anguish, he confessed that his small level of faith in Jesus was being deflected and overcome through the increasing destructive demonic actions upon his son, so he pleads for Christ's intervention.

Nothing can be more touching as this scene. An overwhelmed but loving father, distressed at the condition of his son, having gone to the disciples in vain, now pleading to The Lord and not having the full confidence that he thought he needed to qualify for God's aid, he cries. Any man would have wept in his condition, but the Lord had compassion and exerted His Authority over the situation.

**While the suffering father had been disappointed by the disciples' lack of power, Christ then attributed the disappointment to the lack of faith.** So much rests upon our "believing in faith" and must be backed up with a life of prayer, studying the Holy Scriptures, and fasting, as noted by Jesus' final comments in verse 29.

Now, the same Bible that informs us that Christ came to save sinners and whosoever shall call upon the name of The Lord shall be saved also assures us of The Lord's promise in Matthew 21:21.

**Matthew 21:21 NASB** says, "And Jesus answered and said to them, Truly I say to you if you have faith and do not doubt, you will not only do what was done to the fig tree, but even if you say to this mountain, Be taken up and cast into the sea, it will happen."

**"Having Faith" is placing your confidence in God's Word, believing that He meant what He said, and then walking in obedience and trusting Him.**

**But "Doubting"** means to consider unlikely, to have uncertainties, to be hesitant to believe, to distrust, speak words of unbelief, and be fearful .

Our faith should be predicated in or solely rest on what Christ has said and done, which was vindicated by His Resurrection from that empty tomb. **Placing our confidence in The Living Word of God therefore assures us that through faith our mountains shall become molehills or flattened plains before Him if we don't doubt in our hearts.**

Therefore, no believer should be confused, puzzled, or ever doubtful about this promise from the lips of our Savior.

Believers must remember that the enemy has been rendered powerless and ineffective to destroy those who put their trust in the cross and risen Lord.

**Now, one of the main problems with many believers is that they are still operating in the strength of their own intellect, senses, and emotions, thereby limiting, restricting, and even denying the power of Christ.**

**In John 4:24 NASB, Jesus declared** "God is spirit, and those who worship Him must worship in spirit and truth."

Though His movements are invisible as he orchestrates in our affairs, **believers must learn to trust Him even without any outward sign or visible evidence of His divine hand at work in our lives.** We must learn to stand in faith and trust Him even if things continue to appear the contrary to what we're believing.

We must view Christ as **OUR HOPE** and believe that **HE CARES.** Christ is still on the throne, has **NOT BEEN** caught off guard by your situation, and has complete authority over all that you're facing in this dying world.

**So despite living in these perilous times, have faith in God and keep trusting Him.**

# 22

# "Have You Ever Showed Kindness Only To Be Repaid With Meanness?"

In certain countries, those who show hospitality or kindness to strangers are rewarded, while those who do harm stand in jeopardy of facing a harsh judgment.

During His earthly ministry, Jesus was both a host who received strangers and a guest who received hospitality. So He instructed His disciples to be a blessing wherever they were received.

While we would love to believe that all of our good deeds and godly actions shown to others will result with the same affectionate display back to us, we must remember we are in a world filled with **"spiritual warfare."**

While it's a shame, we must not think it strange if ugly comments, negative remarks or evil railing actions are demonstrated after a display of our generosity and love. Satan is out to deceive us, create strife, promote ill will and give rise to evil reports about believers. He will always attempt to provoke you even to cease in doing good works towards others.

**Whether in the church to other members or unto strangers in the street, we must always remember that any good deed that we render, we do it out of a heart filled with the spirit of love unto Christ and that He alone is the source of our reward.**

**In The Old Testament, in II Samuel Chapter 10,** we are given a special account where David's kindness was misconstrued and repaid with evil.

While we are not told about any special alliance or agreement between David and Nahash, or about the kindness that Nahash showed to David, when Nahash died, David thought to send a delegation to express his condolences to his son, the new king.

**II Samuel 10: 2-4 NIV says that,** David thought, "I will show kindness to Hanun son of Nahash, just as his father showed kindness to me." So David sent a delegation to express his sympathy to Hanun concerning his father. When David's men came to the land of the Ammonites, the Ammonite commanders said to Hanun their lord, "Do you think David is honoring your father by sending envoys to you to express sympathy? Hasn't David sent them to you only to explore the city and spy it out and overthrow it?" So Hanun seized David's envoys, shaved off half of each man's beard, cut off their garments at the buttocks, and sent them away."

David's gesture was sent to do honor to the memory of the passing king and comfort his son doing the loss of his father. **Not only was this an act of sympathy but also a possible attempt to build a new relationship with the new king.** But Hanun and his nobles drew other conclusions, believing that they were spies coming to examine their nation to launch a future attack.

**So instead of treating them with respect, they were man-handled and violated in a shameful and humiliating manner.**

The beard was a mark of being a free and important man, so to cut it off on one side was an insult to David. Additionally, as only the priests wore long underwear, the ordinary dress of men consisted of a tunic and loose flowing robe thrown over it. So the cutting of this robe up to the hip and exposing their buttocks was a vile, shameful and abominable act. In the midst of all of the mourners, they were laughed to scorn. **David had meant peace and friendship, but kindness was not returned.** So David vowed revenge for this public outrage.

What led them to believe that David wasn't sincere? Did they deliberately want to provoke a war? Were they jealous of David's previous military success? Were they harboring grudges against the nation of Israel? **Have you ever showed kindness to someone and they repaid your kindness with evil deeds,**

**slanderous words or actions?  Why do you believe they did this to you and what have you done to forgive them?**

I know that it may naturally appear to be very difficult not to become angry at someone that you've reached out to encourage, befriend, feed and bless and then in return you were treated otherwise.

"Love your enemies, do good to those who hate you, bless those who curse you, pray for those who mistreat you," **were the words from Jesus and they were not a request.**

**For God tells us in Proverbs 25:22,** "In doing this, you will heap burning coals on his head and The Lord will reward you."

**THEREFORE, HAVE FAITH IN GOD!**

# 23

## "Are You Going To Church But Returning Home The Same Way?"

**Do you have questions that need real answers?  Are you in need of a fresh revelation from The Lord?   Are you praying but not seeing answers?   Do you want to see the power of God moving in your life?**

Experiencing the grace and power of God is **MUCH MORE** than just routinely attending a religious service, sitting in a church pew, clapping your hands to the beat of the praise music or saying an occasional **"Amen"** as the pastor preaches.

The Word of God is The Power of God Through Christ Jesus. The same Word that became flesh through the incarnation is very real today through His resurrection. And today, Jesus still saves, forgives, delivers, heals, provides for, comforts, enables and strengthens. **DO YOU KNOW AND BELIEVE HIM?**

**In Acts 8:26-40,** we are given an amazing story in which The Holy Spirit went into great detail to tell us about a man returning home unsatisfied about his religious experience. He was still hungry for the truth.

Returning from Jewish worship services in Jerusalem, **he sat reading a scroll of Isaiah 53: 7-8, with a great desire to know more.** There was still a void in his heart as he left, but God went into action on the dusty road as he was on his way back home.

Philip, who was one of the original deacons selected to serve tables in the church, was now mightily being used by God to evangelize the region by preaching Jesus Christ.

Philip, who wasn't told what to expect, was being divinely guided to go to a desert road as The Lord was supernaturally controlling the events. So upon arrival, he found this Ethiopian Eunuch of great authority sitting in his chariot reading.

When Philip appeared, the Ethiopian Eunuch didn't question Philip about who he was or from where he'd come. He needed something else, **ANSWERS!** Answers that only God could supply.

**So a man of God, full of The Word of God, anointed with The Spirit of God was being used to preach Jesus Christ.**

God had gone and still goes to great lengths for you to know and experience Him. The only question that remains is **"Are you willing to allow Christ to impact your life through His Word and Holy Spirit?"**

**In Acts 8:30-31 NASB, the Bible says,** "Philip ran up and heard him reading Isaiah the prophet, and said, "Do you understand what you are reading?" And he said, "Well, how could I, unless someone guides me?" And he invited Philip to come up and sit with him.

Philip did more than just interpret this portion of scripture, **HE PREACHED JESUS** to this eunuch. He didn't offer any religious philosophy, church traditional views or new age doctrine. **HE PREACHED THE RESURRECTED AND ASCENDED JESUS CHRIST!**

God knows who you are, where you are and what you need most. **If you give Him all of yourself, He will give you all of Himself.**

**"Is your heart hungry for Him?"** What is it that you're missing or lacking? What do you need from The Lord? What void do you have that needs to be filled? What emptiness are you experiencing that needs to be satisfied? What do you need from The Living Christ?

Christ, through His Word and Holy Spirit, wants to move in your heart and life and orchestrate in your affairs. Will you walk with

Him and allow God to do something gracious and amazing that only He can do?

The Jews of that day believed that eunuchs were prohibited from coming into the assembly of God's people because they were regarded as ritually impure **according to Lev. 21: 20 and 22: 19-25.** But Isaiah had prophesied that one day eunuchs would be allowed into the assembly of God's people **in Isaiah 56: 3-5** and that prophecy was fulfilled here in Acts.

So when the eunuch saw there was water near, he asked Philip to baptize him and after making his confession to Christ, Philip didn't hesitate to baptize him.

Finally, upon returning to his chariot, he wasn't troubled that Philip was snatched away by The Spirit of God; it didn't seem to bother him. For he now had come to experience the Risen Christ and kept on rejoicing as he went on his way back home.

# 24

## "Bitter or Better –
## Which Road Have You Chosen?"

Many years ago there was a famous TV show which featured a man named **"Archie Bunker,"** whose life simply oozed bitterness, ignorance and foolishness.

Upon watching it, one might start to wonder where we would be if the misbehaving people would start using their negative and destructive energies to do good things, to enhance and better our world.

Now, while I know that we don't live in a **"dream world,"** there is a lot of potential for greater things to occur if more walked in the light of Christ instead of living in darkness.

But there's a greater issue at stake here because **there are countless people who claim that they've been delivered out of darkness through Jesus Christ, but they're still allowing the spirit of darkness to control their thinking and actions** towards others. And one of the ways is in the area of **"bitterness."**

**The Holy Spirit of God reveals in Proverbs 16:32 that,** "He who is slow to anger is better than the mighty, and he who rules his spirit, than he who captures a city."

**People led by God's Spirit are bridge builders and not destroyers of life. They are lifters of heads and not the breakers of backs. So, which one are you?**

Now, there's more to distinguishing these two words than just one vowel being different in them. **The Holy Spirit of God wants you to realize that your road cannot or will not get better if you remain bitter in your heart before God.**

Do you know that a person whose heart is right before God using wisdom can accomplish much more than he ever could by just using physical force or brute strength?

Did you know that a wise man's words uttered calmly **are of more value than** the one who seeks to force his ways upon others through loudness and unwise instruction?

**Ecclesiastes 9: 17-18 NTL says,** "Better to hear the quiet words of a wise person than the shouts of a foolish king. Better to have wisdom than weapons of war, but one sinner can destroy much that is good."

**Now some of the main characteristics or traits of a person filled with bitterness are** anger, hostility, hatefulness, antagonism, bearing grudges, resentment, miserable, wickedness, negativity, scornfulness, full of stinging criticism, sour in life, harshness, unforgiving, disagreeable and destructive.

Not only can a bitter person bring destruction upon his own soul but their corruption, bad example, mischief and foolish counsel **can have devastating effects upon the family, neighborhood, nation and even a church.**

Now, the word **"better"** is used 218 times throughout scripture and some of the main characteristics or traits of the word **"better"** are: a morally superior quality, virtuousness, a spirit of excellence, improved in wisdom, joyfulness and having a more appropriate or acceptable way or manner. These individuals seek to amend, advance, promote, correct, reform and rectify circumstances, situations and relationships.

**The Holy Spirit of God instructs us in Hebrews 12: 14-15 NIV to,** "Make every effort to live in peace with everyone and to be holy; without holiness no one will see the Lord. See to it that no one falls short of the grace of God and that no bitter root grows up to cause trouble and defile many."

**So, if you want to walk in the favor of God, make sure you choose the right road and allow the peace and grace of The Lord to rule and reign in your life.**

# 25

## "What Should You Do When You Come To The End Of Your Rope?"

**When people come to the end of the rope,** why don't they seek God first, in faith with confidence in His Word, instead of searching for alternative solutions through exhaustive, fleshly, and even extremely costly means?

**Why do people, especially believers, explore so many other options before putting The Lord first?** When did seeking Christ and the grace of God become a last resort?

**"If you've tried everything but nothing seems to work, then try Jesus."** While these were the opening words of a song I used to sing in a choir many years ago, over the years it's seemed to trouble my heart to a great degree and began to make me asks questions.

**Considering God as a last resort always results with a loss of time, missed opportunities, delayed breakthroughs, financial loss, family division, and experiencing unnecessary heartaches, hurt and pain.**

Additionally, considering God as a last resort can be a sign or a symptom of even a more serious problem: **SIN!** This is not a time for selective amnesia, doubt, unbelief, or walking in the flesh, but time to look to Jesus Christ and stand up in faith.

Have you forgotten just how much He loves you and takes delight in demonstrating His power and grace in the midst of His children? **Can you agree that there's nothing too hard for Him to do?**

**1st Peter 5:6-7 says,** "Humble yourselves, therefore, under God's mighty hand, that he may lift you up in due time. Cast all your anxiety on him because he cares for you."

The entire plan of Satan is to bring enough pain and heartache into your life to crush your faith in Christ and produce ruin and total destruction. **But are there any difficulties that faith in The Living Savior cannot cure, remedy, heal, or deliver?**

You are encouraged and instructed to cast all your care: personal care, family care, financial care, cares for the present, cares for the future, care for others, care for your society and care for your church, **all on God.**

Failure to do this will produce greater heartache, misery, doubt, anguish and unbelief, which always will distract the mind and lead to sin. The only remedy is to cast all your care upon God and leave everything to His Divine and Gracious Intervention.

**Remember the wonderful promising words of Jesus that He spoke in Matthew 6:33,** "Seek ye first the kingdom of God and his righteousness and all these things shall be added unto you."

There are so many biblical stories where God entered into seemingly impossible situations involving an individual, a family, group, or a nation, where He mightily intervened and rendered salvation, healing, deliverance, provision, a blessing or a victory to those that looked to Him.

**So, now this is your hour to trust Him even if you can't see what He's doing or understand how He's orchestrating in your affairs at this very moment.** Cast all your cares upon Him. Hang it all on His Cross. Know that Jesus died for you. But even more importantly, know that **He Arose for you** and in and through Him you can now be victorious.

**THEREFORE, HAVE FAITH IN GOD!**

# 26

## "Will The Real Believers Today, Please Stand Up?"

In a world filled with fake money, phony love, empty promises, folks hopping from one church to another and counterfeit believers, how can people come to know the real thing?

**What does it take to stand up in a world that's fallen down? What main characteristic is The Lord looking for in the lives of people that are called by His Name?** Whenever God is looking for a person to use, He examines their heart because your heart is the point of connection to Him.

Besides faith, The Lord is searching for surrender, submission, commitment and determination in the hearts and lives of those that will truly walk with Him and stand on His word.

**Have you made a choice between eternal treasures or worldly pleasures? Have you made the decision to stand up and be counted for God?**

**An excellent example of this can be found in the book of Daniel. Daniel 1:8 informs us,** "But Daniel purposed in his heart that he would not defile himself with the portion of the king's meat, nor with the wine which he drank: therefore he requested of the prince of the eunuchs that he might not defile himself."

The Babylonian food, it's prior usage in idol worship and it unclean preparation did not conform to the Old Testament teachings. Knowing that the food and wine were connected with idolatry and forbidden by The Law given to Moses, inconsistent with his principles, against his morals, perilous to his welfare and just plain wrong before God, Daniel purposed in his heart and made up his mind to discipline his body, stand up in faith and not defile himself.

True believers know that we are **"in the world but not part of this worldly system."** Daniel may have lived in Babylon, but he took special care to ensure that **"the spirit of Babylon"** would not take over or control his heart.

**Can the world look at you today and see the difference?** If a believer becomes so worldly, what good is their witness or testimony of God before the unbelievers?

Not willing to have an attitude of open defiance and provoke harsh opposition, Daniel made a simple but humble request to the jail keeper in charge; that he might be permitted for 10 days to eat certain mixed vegetables and drink water, then be examined after their experiment to see if they appeared healthy and strong as if they had eaten their foods. And God granted him special favor with the jailor. Then at the conclusion of the trial period, they were even healthier and stronger than expected.

**When your response is shaped by God's Word and Holy Spirit, you too will begin to experience the grace and favor of God in your midst when you make the decision to stand up in Christ.**

Daniel stood out like an oasis in the desert. Just like Moses, Daniel and his three friends chose rather to suffer affliction with the people of God, rather than to enjoy the pleasures of sin for a season.

**It's extremely vital for people to understand that those who will honor God under any situation, God in return will wonderfully honor them.**

**THEREFORE, HAVE FAITH IN GOD!**

# 27

# "Do You Believe That Someone Else Is Responsible For Your Situation?"

Casting the blame onto others or **"passing the buck"** is quite common in our world since the beginning of time. **It's a person's fleshly, sinful and cowardly act of failing to take the responsibility for one's very own wrongful act as they attempt to attribute it to another person or group.**

History has revealed many young people blaming their parents and many parents blaming their society for the lack of values or good upbringing. Our political arena is in shambles because each political party accuses the other instead of seeking a common ground for the benefit of all the people.

How many husbands have had affairs because they tried to blame their spouse for being cold, unloving, uninterested or no longer able to satisfy their emotional and sexual needs. While Satan's temptations are attractive, they are deceptive and destructive, **for the Bible still says that the wages of sin is death. (Romans 6:23)**

The rich continue to blame the poor and the poor blame the rich for the ill conditions in our society. Bigotry and gender bias is on the rise again as situations are about to re-ignite on the scene with everyone pointing the finger at the other person or group. **Then if that's not enough, recently in the news, a convicted murderer tried to blame his evil activities on the fast foods and pastries that he had earlier consumed!**

Rather than holding yourself personally accountable and seeking forgiveness, deliverance, healing and guidance, many attempts to just cast the blame on others to ascribe or cover up their sins. **But God holds each personally responsible for their own disobedience, failures, sins and lack of faith.**

For The Lord has given you **"the power of choice."** Now as God seeks to influence your choices, Satan also seeks to influence your actions and decisions. God has created man to be a free moral agent, whose individual decisions will determine his destiny. **Such was the case way back in the Garden of Eden.**

God created Adam and Eve and placed them in a paradise environment with the simple instructions **NOT** to eat from the tree of the knowledge of good and evil, for in the day they would, they would die. **(Genesis 2:17)**

Once Eve was tempted and ate the forbidden fruit, she quickly turned to Adam and he, not weakened, impaired or deceived, immediately, knowingly and deliberately ate of the same fruit. **Adam plainly showed contempt for what God had done for him by placing a higher value on his relationship with his wife than on his relationship and communion with his creator.**

**Then Genesis 3:7 NIV says**, "Then the eyes of both of them were opened, and they realized they were naked; so they sewed fig leaves together and made coverings for themselves." **Then they ran and even tried to hide from God.**

**Then in Genesis 3:9,** God calls out, **"Adam, where are you?"** Adam and Eve did not manage to hide themselves in a place where God couldn't see them, for where can you go to avoid His Presence? **NO, this indicates that God wanted them to bring themselves out as He came searching for those who were now lost.** But out of disobedience, they were now afraid of God's holiness. **Before they sinned they welcomed God's gracious visits with joy, but now He was a terror to them.**

Their answers to God's questions only revealed that neither was willing to accept that they had failed. Adam no longer referred to Eve as **"bone of my bone and flesh of my flesh"** but pointed the finger at her and now blamed God for her presence and actions.

**Genesis 3: 12-13 NIV says,** "The man said, the woman you put here with me, she gave me some fruit from the tree, and I ate it." Then the LORD God said to the woman, **"What is this you have done?"** The woman said, "The serpent deceived me, and I ate."

Adam and Eve both tried to excuse the sin by laying the blame and shame on others. **Satan may tempt, but he cannot force you to do anything contrary to your will.** He may suggest, persuade or entice you to sin but he cannot **"make"** you do it. If his subtlety draws you into sin, then you must rightfully admit to your sinful activities.

When a child messes up and honestly comes and admits it, what loving parent would not forgive and embrace the child? There may be a punishment, yes, but that only serves to strengthen the child's character. **How much more will your loving Father in Heaven, who gave His only Son to die for your sins, embrace and love you?**

The final question is, will you run away from the Father's immense loving forgiveness by trying to shift the blame, **when He who knows all and sees all, already knows the truth?**

# 28

## "Are You Longing For A Change But One Doesn't Appear Anywhere In Sight?"

I began conversing with a woman that I knew was experiencing hard times when suddenly she looked at me and out of anguish said, **"I'm still waiting for my ship to come in!"** So, to lighten the moment, I jokingly replied, **"It did, but it sank in the harbor! And if you want your stuff you'll have to dive down to get it and I'll help you."** This brought great laughter to her depressed and discouraged face.

Longing for a change, something better or different always seems to be a driving factor in our lives, with disappointments running a close second in the race. But, the Bible offers us more than a theology for overcoming a variety of situations.

**Psalms 46:1 says,** "God is our refuge and strength, a very present help in trouble."

During any **"soul-shaking"** experience, in the midst of the worst of times, we are helpless without Christ. It's during these encounters or attacks that **HE IS** our fortitude, salvation, deliverance, guidance, comfort and help even in our darkest hour. **Do you believe this?**

God is our source to flee to for safety, strength, shelter, aid and assistance despite any danger, trouble or even weakness that may come our way. **HE IS** the strength for our hearts under the greatest of trials and our **"way out of no way"** from every enemy that surrounds us. **Again, do you believe this?**

The words **"Present Help"** reveals that **HE IS** the proven, powerful, effectual, reliable and faithful ONE. **HE ALONE** makes the difference because of who **HE IS** and the grace that

He loves to demonstrate in the lives of those that trust Him and confess Him before all others.

The word **"Trouble"** identifies all that will come upon us which will bring sorrow, anxiety, discouragement, broken-heartedness and grief.

**God is the God of all comfort and He has a lengthy and faithful history of divinely intervening and orchestrating in our affairs.** Now is **NOT** the time to give up on God because **HE HAS NOT** given up on you.

While the gospel is the Good News to the world, too much Christian teaching today seems to be a little more than positivism plastered with religious jargon or clichés. We must cease preaching **"faith in our faith"** and recover the distinctive ability to have faith in **THE LIVING CHRIST** and His atoning work, walk in obedience to the scriptures and listen to the voice of The Holy Spirit.

Remember that Christ **IS THE LORD OF YOUR BREAKTHROUGH**, so you don't have anything to fear!

**THEREFORE, HAVE FAITH IN GOD!**

# 29

## "What Steps Should You Take To Keep The Fire Burning?"

While an out of control wildfire can have devastating effects in our environment, fire controlled and properly used has great advantages. Fire cooks food, sterilizes medical instruments, boils water, heats homes, welds metal, refines gold and purifies against bacteria. Fire is one of the most forceful and needed natural elements in our world which, if properly used, can manufacture or produce change.

**So, in 2nd Timothy 1:6, The Apostle Paul instructed Timothy to** "Stir up the gift of God that is within you," because he knew that the word **"stir"** means to **"fan the flames of the fire."**

Evidently Timothy was struggling with discouragement from imprisonment or from facing other imminent dangers, so Paul wrote to encourage and strengthen him. **Therefore, that which Christ has placed inside of you, that which you've been called to do, "STIR IT UP!"**

Paul exhorts Timothy to stand fast on God's Holy Scriptures and to stir up the gift of God within him through the laying on of The Apostle's hand, under the anointing of The Holy Spirit, when he was ordained by God.

The gift that Timothy had received was **The Holy Spirit,** and through Him, he received the anointing and the power to preach and teach the gospel of Jesus Christ.

While Timothy, like so many believers today, didn't possess the tenacious or relentless zeal of The Apostle, **Paul urged him to unleash the invincible power of God's Spirit against all the various storms that will come to rise against us.**

**Like Timothy, we are to rekindle the fire, blow on the coals, cause the flames to burn more brightly, be more zealous about what Christ has set you apart to do and keep adding more fuel to the fire.**

You do these things by keeping your mind renewed through The Word of God, fellowshipping with Christ, remaining prayerful. Keep piercing through the darkness, not quenching The Holy Spirit, listening to some inspirational gospel music and good Bible messages. Recall what God has done in your past and read some inspiring articles and testimonies about what God is doing through the lives of others around the world.

God has not given us a spirit of fear, but of faith, love, courage and power to face and handle all the difficulties, dangers and adversities that will come our way.

**When your flesh or the devil attempts to extinguish the fire within your heart, do all that you can to keep it ignited and burning.**

If there is no fire, then there will be no excitement, no joy, no enthusiasm, no hope and no anointing. You can't touch the lives of others around you with a discouraged, broken-hearted, depressed and defeated soul.

But underneath those gray, dusty ashes, there's still a spark that God's able to set ablaze again if you're willing to start **"fanning the flames within you."**

**In Jeremiah chapter 20, the prophet grew weary and became so discouraged regarding the insults and the injuries that he was experiencing until he privately declared that he wouldn't preach or prophesy anymore. In His heart he even said, "I will not make mention of Him nor speak His name anymore."**

Jeremiah's flesh, along with the devil's attacks to his mind, convinced him that every time he spoke, his conditions worsen. So as he attempted to take off his prophet's robe, lay aside the Old Testament scrolls, cease, refrain, stop preaching and quench

The Spirit of God, the Word of God burned so hot and deep within his soul until he screamed, **"It's like a fire, shut up in my bones! And I cannot hold it in"** (Read Jeremiah 20:9)

It doesn't matter what happened to diminish or put the fire out in your life. Persecution, criticism, depression, burnout, sickness, divorce, abusiveness, financial hardships, an unforeseen event or accident or even the death of a loved one.

You will never recover, rise up or reach your potential unless you **"fan the flames of the gift of God that's within you."**

**THEREFORE, HAVE FAITH IN GOD!**

# 30

# "Aren't You Glad You Don't Look Like What You've Been Through?"

As a believer in Christ, I've personally discovered that **"while we've been through hell, we don't have to look like the hell that we've been through."** God is still in the business of bringing us out of the fire without any outward evidence that you've ever been in the flames.

When I was a young teenager, one of the first things that I noticed about the older saints in my church was how much joy they had despite all the hardships they testified that they've been through. Then I noticed they appeared more **"radiant"** than those that were outside of Christ who were going through very similar circumstances.

Over the many years since, while I've learned that no one is exempt from **"the school of hard knocks,"** those who trust Christ and are led by The Spirit of God are on a journey from **"being a victim to having the victory."**

**Psalms 30:5b says** "....weeping may endure for a night, but joy *cometh* in the morning." When trials and afflictions are the most severe, pressing or heavily upon us, **we rejoice that we are comforted by His promises in His Word. We also know that His Light cannot and never will be overcome with darkness.**

Despite what believers are going through, we rejoice because of all the great things that The Lord has done and what we believe by faith that he will do.

So instead of looking stressed out, beat down, worn out, despondent and talking defeat, believers realize that **"though we be cast down we will not be destroyed"** and maintain hope eternal as we go through any fiery trial surrounding us.

We believe that we too shall be brought **"Up From The Ashes"** just like the 3 Hebrews in Daniel chapter 3. We place our full confidence in His Promise as quoted in Hebrews 13:5, **"That I Will Never Leave Thee and Never Forsake Thee."** Believers constantly sing songs of encouragement that **"this too shall pass."**

Just this past week, I met a wonderful and dynamic man of God who was really praising The Lord. **This anointed minister briefly shared his testimony that he had undergone two kidney transplants and because his body rejected them, he went into a coma for 90 days.**

While others made plans for his funeral, the saints of God kept praying. He's now taking daily medication to keep his kidneys properly functioning but he's rejoicing all over the church. **He has this huge, radiant, glowing and smiling face as he's walking, talking, preaching and encouraging people everywhere about the love of Christ.** There wasn't any outward physical evidence showing that he'd ever recently been through that ordeal.

**Yes, while we've been through hell, we don't have to look like the hell that we've been through."** Again I say that God is still in the business of bringing us out of the fire without any outward evidence that you've been in the flames.

**THEREFORE, HAVE FAITH IN GOD!**

# 31

## "Are You Allowing Uncertainty To Crush Your Heart And Rob You?"

On different occasions doubt, uncertainty, skepticism, indecision, insecurity or instability has arisen in the hearts and minds of God's people to trouble or perplex them regarding God's power and His promises during difficult times.

But, nothing should be allowed to give us such a lack of assurance or separate us from the love, grace and the promises of Our Living Savior & Lord, Jesus Christ. **No, not even death itself.**

To help us be reminded of this, **let's reconsider the story in Matthew 14: 22-36 of Peter walking upon the water.** After struggling and exhausting themselves to keep their boat afloat on the sea during a turbulent storm, Jesus goes to their rescue by the means of walking on the water. But when they see Him coming, they're even more afraid believing him to be a ghost.

So Jesus calls out to them, identifying Himself and tells them not to fear. Peter responses, **"If it is you then permit me to come to you."** Jesus said, **"Come"** and Peter began to walk on the water towards Christ.

**Then Matthew 14: 30-31 says,** "But when he saw the wind, he was afraid and, beginning to sink, cried out, "Lord, save me!" Immediately Jesus reached out his hand and caught him. "You of little faith," **He said,** "Why did you doubt?"

In this familiar story Peter, being upheld by the power of Christ, walked upon the water not for any personal gain but to go to Jesus. As long as his full focus remained on Jesus, he was wonderfully borne up. But when Peter saw and felt the strong hard wind blowing against him and the violent waves of the sea increasing to rise, his eyes became distracted and his attention diverted away from Jesus, who initially was empowering him to walk on top of those opposing conditions.

Even in our worst or most severe stormy days, **HE IS OUR VERY PRESENT HELP.** Our dependence should be on Christ. **For He's far greater and more superior than any hard time, negative situation , painful condition or demonic activity that you could ever encounter or experience.**

To show the greatness of His love, mercy, power and grace, various adversities will arise in our lives to often tempt, discourage, oppose, defeat and even try to destroy us but special promises and grace have been given to all, whose eyes remain focused on Christ.

It was through **FAITH** in Jesus that Peter was being supernaturally and divinely upheld, but when that faith wavered, the laws of gravitation were re-activated during his supernatural walk and then he began to quickly sink. The violent winds and raging sea may have distracted his attention away, **but it was the reduction of his faith that caused him to quickly sink and endanger his life.**

After saving his life, The Lord rebuked Peter for his weakness of faith in allowing doubt to prevail to rob him of blessing. **For there is no good reason why Christ's believers today should be of a doubtful mind when we've been given so great a salvation with so many assurances.**

According to the Word of God, we should always expect our Lord's divine intervention into our lives and affairs through faith. We should trust that His almighty outstretched arms will rescue and deliver us in every situation.

Satan will speak to your heart and minds in an attempt to distract, divert, discourage and depress your mind and crush your spirit as you face the circumstances in your life. **But don't allow doubt and unbelief to rob you of the blessings and victory God wants you to experience through Christ.**

Know that the cure for doubt and unbelief in all situations is to keep your mind and heart renewed in The Word and Promises of God. Learn God's Word, renew it in your heart, recite it daily, meditate on it day and night, never let it depart from you **and your life will be descriptive of Psalm 1: 3, which says** "And he shall be like a tree planted by the rivers of water, that bringeth forth his fruit in his season; his leaf also shall not wither; and whatsoever he doeth shall prosper."

**THEREFORE, HAVE FAITH IN GOD!**

# 32

# "How Does God Bring Order Out Of Disorder?"

**It's important for us today to remember that the Christian Life is an ongoing fight against the forces of darkness.** It's also important for us to remember that when Christ makes us victorious in any area, it doesn't mean that we won't face any future battles or hurdles.

So you need to remind yourself to remain strong in faith, diligent in prayer and keep God's word in front of you in order to experience the grace of God and The Holy Spirit orchestrating in your life and affairs. For it has been said that **"when praises go up, blessings come down."** Nothing is ever the same as you learn to trust God and turn things over to Him.

**In 2 Chronicles Chapter 15, we're given the amazing account of Asa, the King of Judah, who was returning from the battlefield.** God had just given Judah the victory over their enemy when a prophet came out from Jerusalem to meet the returning victorious king with a special prophetic word from The Lord.

**2 Chronicles 15: 1-2 NIV says,** "The Spirit of God came on Azariah son of Oded. He went out to meet Asa and said to him, "Listen to me Asa and all Judah and Benjamin. The LORD is with you when you are with him. If you seek him, he will be found by you, but if you forsake him, he will forsake you."

The nation of Judah had earlier sinned, turning it's back on God and had given itself over to idolatry. Suddenly, the nation of Ethiopia began to rise up and come against Judah just as Asa was made the new king.

Judah was greatly outnumbered but King Asa and the people turned to God in prayer. Rather than attempting any strategic military plan, they humbled themselves before The Lord and God wonderfully gave them the victory over their enemy, which was more than twice their size.

**God not only gave Judah the victory over that nation, but fear also came upon all the other surrounding nations that God was with them.**

Now Asa is met by this Prophet of God with a message that **"God has helped them"** with a new call or word of encouragement **"to obedience."**

As long as they stood with God, followed His commandments and worshipped Him, they would be blessed in seeing the hand of God moving in their midst. **But the same message from the prophet also sounded a danger warning of abandoning God and abdicating faith in His word.**

So often, the forces of darkness will try to get believers **"to relax and let down their guard"** especially after being exhausted from a hard struggle or at the end of a stressful day. The devil believes that's a good opportunity for him to remind you of your physical, emotional or material needs, in an attempt to distract, persuade or lead you off course.

**In our weakest hour or most exhaustive condition, we should always remember that The Holy Spirit is ever present to be our comfort and strength.** Christ wants us to praise Him from our hearts, keep our minds renewed in His word, keep our faith in Him and remain focused.

The prophet's message was so accepted by King Asa that he began to make drastic changes and reforms throughout the entire kingdom of Judah. He even pronounced a death penalty on anyone who didn't honor The Law and obey God's covenant, starting with his very own grandmother.

**Does God Have Your Heart? Are you walking in His Grace? Are you seeking His face through prayer?** He has promised that He would never leave or forsake you but have you made the same commitment to Him?

Many today are in the trouble that they're experiencing because they've turned their back on God. When you leave your first love and abandon the biblical principles of The Lord, you'll end up suffering the consequences of **"reaping what you sown."**

All those that turn to God and trust Him will discover that the Lord shall be your helper as you continue to walk in his ways.

**THEREFORE, HAVE FAITH IN GOD!**

# 33

# "Have You Ever Felt Like Giving Up As You Waited On The Lord?"

Whenever hard times, negative situations, and painful conditions arise in our midst, **we must believe to see, not see to believe,** that our Lord will mightily move in our lives. You must remember that wherever a believer is, he or she can always find a way to the throne of grace through prayer and trusting God for His Divine Intervention.

**Today, many only feel like giving up because they don't sense God's presence as they're focusing on their gloomy situation instead of giving Christ their undivided attention, standing on God's Word, and listening to the voice of The Holy Spirit.** But The Lord wants to enlarge your testimony and mature your faith as you learn to prevail and pierce through the darkness around you. For this is not the time to give up, **but your hour to BELIEVE HIM!**

**Now, a special word of assurance and encouraging testimony is found in Psalms 27:13 where David said,** "I would have fainted, unless I had believed to see the goodness of the LORD in the land of the living."

Evil had raised its hand as many false witnesses rose up against David and threatened to destroy both his life and the lives of his friends. The opposition was so numerous, mighty and fierce that everything physically appeared helpless, hopeless, useless and that death was at hand.

David said that his only support was his faith in God and his belief that he would yet be permitted to see the goodness of God upon the earth. **Here David does not speak of faith that he once had, but of the faith, confidence, and assurance that he now has. But, in what was this confidence grounded ?**

He believed, trusted and relied on The Word and The Promises of God. Then with this deep internal conviction, he had the fullest belief that God would intervene to save, heal, provide and change his present circumstances by delivering him out of the hands of his enemies.

**His faith in God was sufficient enough to calm his mind and sustain him under those stressful and heart-wrenching conditions.** This psalm clearly revealed David's state of heart and mind despite the efforts of his enemies to destroy him. David firmly believed in God's Presence, and by seeking His Face, he was trusting God for His Divine Guidance and His Almighty Invisible Protection. As the result of this God brought great deliverance and victory into His life.

In times of affliction, perplexity, and discouragement, **you too can have this same assurance because of God's Love, Grace and Power promised to all believers through His Word and by His Holy Spirit.**

Waiting on The Lord does not mean sitting idle on your living room sofa or a park bench just hoping for anything to happen in your midst. **NO!** Waiting on The Lord means standing in faith and waiting with great expectation. Waiting on The Lord means that you're praising God for having heard your prayer and thanking Him in advance for His Divine Intervention.

Waiting on The Lord means **"Standing In Faith"** and standing is an act of aggression and strength. Waiting on The Lord means that you're piercing through the darkness in prevailing prayer as you're standing in faith. **Standing In Faith means that you are refusing to accept circumstances or the conditions the way they are** and you are believing God for great changes, according to His promises in His Word.

As you look to Our Mighty Savior and Lord Jesus Christ, through fervent prayer and faith, you too can be delivered from the hands of the enemy that's oppressing you. So remain encouraged and wait on the Lord with great expectation with the full assurance that God will also mightily intervene in your life.

# 34

# "Did You Know That God Can Use People Even When They Don't Know That They're Being Used By Him?"

As you study the scriptures, one of the most important revelations that will help you grow in your walk with God is **"There's Nothing Too Hard For God To Do."** As The Holy Spirit constantly orchestrates and moves in our world, Christ touches the lives of others around you to impact, influence, affect and even bless your life. Yes, even if they're not aware of the invisible presence of God impacting their thoughts or actions in relationship to you, God is using them.

**In 1ˢᵗ Samuel, Chapter 29, we read an account that is a wonderful example of this in the life of David.** Out of his fear of King Saul, David and his men had fled from Israel and moved into the land of the Philistines, who were their enemy. For over 15 months, David lived in their land and worked hard to convince the Philistine King that he was now his trusted friend and loyal subject. And King Achish believed David.

But a war soon began to arise between the Philistines and Israel, and David was expected to show his allegiance to the Philistines by fighting for them. King Achish commanded David to mobilize his men to help fight alongside the Philistines, against David's own beloved Israel.

**David had placed himself in a very difficult predicament. He knew if he opposed Israel, he would be standing against The Lord.** As David was nervously trying to figure a way out of his situation, God allowed certain Philistine commanders to remember David's prior victories over them. They became extremely unhappy about David's presence in their midst and demanded that King Achish **NOT** include David in his plans, in case his heart might still be with Israel, and he would sabotage them.

**1ˢᵗ Samuel 29:3-4 NIV says,** "The commanders of the Philistines asked, "What about these Hebrews?" Achish replied, "Is this not David, who was an officer of Saul, King of Israel? He has already been with me for over a year, and from the day he left Saul until now, I have found no fault in him." But the Philistine commanders were angry with Achish and said, "Send the man back, that he may return to the place you assigned him. He must not go with us into battle, or he will turn against us during the fighting. How better could he regain his master's favor than by taking the heads of our own men?""

God had divinely intervened by using the Philistine commanders to deliver David and his soldiers from a very dangerous predicament. God had prevented him from making a costly mistake, without the Philistines even knowing that they were being used by God. **God supernaturally moved upon the hearts of others, thereby saving David from making war against his own country.**

Often a believer will find himself in the very midst of a difficult situation or painful experience where his only solution is the divine intervention of God, through the favor and grace of The Lord. **Remember: When God is all you have, God is all you need.**

We must learn to take comfort in knowing that, whatever is happening to us, God has not been caught off-guard, He is still in full control and is directing things for our good. **We may not always understand or even enjoy some of the things we may have to experience.** But we must stand firm in the truth that things have been designed for our good through Christ, who loves us.

God is in charge. The Holy Spirit of God can touch the hearts of those around you to cause them to be a blessing, or to harden others' hearts so you will be moved where you need to be in order to receive from Him. God is not limited.

**The same power that touches or softens hearts can also bind hands or harden thoughts against you.** But it's still God, mightily moving in your very midst, who is divinely orchestrating your affairs.

**Romans 8:28 NASB says,** "And we know that in all things God works for the good of those who love him, who have been called according to his purpose."

Even if a believer steps out of faith like David did, God will supernaturally intervene and employ certain corrective measures to save, protect, deliver, provide for or set you free.

So, whatever's going on in your life, **God will demonstrate His mercy and grace! He will do whatever it takes** to deliver you out of sin, draw you nearer to Christ, open up wonderful doors, move upon the hearts of others, or separate you from the world as He works to prepare you for eternity with Him.

**THEREFORE, HAVE FAITH IN GOD!**

# 35

## "Have You Ever Had A Dream But Never Acted On It?"

**Have you ever had good intentions but never took the first step towards implementing them?**  Before your dreams become lost and irretrievable, isn't it time for you to be healed and spiritually refreshed so you can recapture your vision and find greater purpose and fulfilled joy?

**Wherever you find yourself in life, there is always room for improvements.  And God is now calling you to go forward because He has something more for you.**

It doesn't matter what you have achieved, accomplished or attained, there's an exciting new challenge ahead for you with new victories to be won.  So you need to be pursuing a dream that God has placed within your heart.

**In Deuteronomy 1: 6 & 8, God said to Moses and Israel,** "You have stayed at this mountain long enough.  It is time to break camp and move on.  Go…  Look, I Am giving all this land to you."

God spoke to Moses at Mt. Horeb and told him that the nation of Israel had stayed too long at that place and that it was time to arise and move forward.

**For one year they sat at the foot of that mountain after their departure from Egypt.**  Even though there they had received The Law, made The Tabernacle, and they were all numbered and prepared for battle, **they had grown used to where they were; perhaps even thinking it was their permanent home.**  But God ordered them to move onward because God had something else greater and better in store for them:  **"The Promised Land."**

Just like the Israelites, too many believers become accustomed to their daily routine or rut. **You have become too used to the place that The Lord only wanted you to pass through, but never to remain.** He has something far greater, glorious, awesome and more exciting in store for you. It's now time to arise because you can't get there unless you first leave where you are.

It's time for you to arise and step out in faith and leave the place of certainty for uncertainty. It's time to launch out into the deep and leave your familiar place or comfort zone, for you have sat where you are too long.

Now Christ has given believers everything that we'll ever need to face every new challenge and spiritual battle on this side of eternity. **All you need to do is to allow The Holy Spirit to direct your path, believe His Word, step out in faith, begin to do the things that you've envisioned, stop making excuses and never look back.**

Remember, you'll never achieve unless you fully believe. And it's God's Will for you to go forward and possess new lands.

**THEREFORE, HAVE FAITH IN GOD!**

# 36

## "What Does It Mean To Be Kept From Dangers Seen And Unseen?"

I quickly turned around as I heard the tip of the gun barrel as it rested on the car window as it was being pointed straight at me......

**I was a street evangelist and a working pastor of a small church in the Compton, Watts and The Inner City of South Central Los Angeles, California.** During those years I had many different experiences in my ministry and life as I took God's word and the gospel of Jesus Christ into the streets and various homes throughout that community.

I awoke early that morning as usual with God's praises softly being sung from my lips not trying to awake my sleeping family as I prepared for work. As I locked my front door, I took a long walk down my driveway to my pick-up truck which was parked out on the street.

It was a dark but very quiet 5am morning and as usual I kept an open eye on all my surroundings. **All seemed perfectly calm and peaceful as I continued singing praises to The Lord as began to unlock my truck.**

Just as I put my key into the door to unlock it, I suddenly heard the sound of something metal tap on the glass and I quickly turned around to see the tip of a gun resting on a slightly lowered, dark tinted window of a car being driven without the headlights on.

Quickly elevating both my arms and hands, I immediately shouted, **"Wait, wait, I'm an older man with little children and I'm on my way to work!"** My red coat being opened because of my elevated arms revealed my job uniform shirt and my I.D. Badge dangling from my shirt collar.

Suddenly, I heard a few voices whispering in the darkened car, then one of the unseen persons said, **"Alright old dude, get rid of that coat!"** With that, the gun disappeared and just as they had come, they quickly sped off into the darkness of the night.

Even though Satan was out to destroy someone that morning through a cowardly drive-by shooting, evidently the color of my coat drew attention to me as it represented the color of a rival gang.

While I had previous encounters dealing with gang activity, street violence and other types of hostility and demonic activity, this was totally different. For like an unforeseen tragic car accident or unexpected life threatening sickness or disease, **I DIDN'T SEE IT COMING.**

**Immediately, The Holy Spirit brought to my remembrance the insightful words found in 1 Peter 1:5-7 NLT ,** "And through your faith, God is protecting you by his power until you receive this salvation, which is ready to be revealed on the last day for all to see. So be truly glad. There is wonderful joy ahead, even though you have to endure many trials for a little while. These trials will show that your faith is genuine. It is being tested as fire tests and purifies gold--though your faith is far more precious than mere gold. So when your faith remains strong through many trials, it will bring you much praise and glory and honor on the day when Jesus Christ is revealed to the whole world."

**The power of God kept me from both dangers seen and unseen.** The ones seen are bad enough, so we can't even begin to imagine the unseen warfare that's going on in the spirit realm all around us.

As Satan and the forces of darkness organize and attempt to set up bad or negative situations, temptations, pitfalls, ungodly plots, wicked entrapments and demonic activity, it's vitally important to remember who we are in Christ and the awesome power of praise.

**Do you believe in guardian angels? Do you believe in God's Divine Intervention and Protection? Do you believe in the awesome presence, power, grace and the Almighty Prevailing Hand of God?**

The sweet smelling aroma of true worshipping praise ascending up into the throne room of God results in yokes being broken, demonic set-ups uncovered and destroyed and bridges being built over troubled waters throughout the storms in your life.

So regardless of whether the dangers are visibly seen or unseen, **walk in the Spirit and lift up your voice before the Lord Jesus Christ and continually give Him the highest praise.** Then you too will realize that you're being kept by His Grace and Power for His purpose.

**THEREFORE, HAVE FAITH IN GOD!**

# 37

# "Are You Aware That Prayer Doesn't Make Things Easy, But It Always Makes Things Change?"

**Have You Really Asked The Lord To Help You?** There are many different Scriptures throughout the Bible that encourage believers that are experiencing a variety of stressful circumstances and painful situations to **PRAY.**

While prayer is one of the most talked about subjects in Christian circles, it's the least performed or often conducted with the wrong motives. **God declares in James 4: 2-3 NIV that** "You desire but do not have, so you kill. You covet but you cannot get what you want, so you quarrel and fight. You do not have because you do not ask God. When you ask, you do not receive, because you ask with wrong motives, that you may spend what you get on your pleasures."

But, with correct motivation, Jesus gave us one of the greatest promises for obtaining whatever we need as He was concluding His Sermon On The Mount. **In Matthew 7:7 Jesus said,** "Ask, and it will be given to you; seek, and you will find; knock, and it will be opened to you."

Here, our Lord not only encourages us to pray but promises that God will respond to our petitions. While prayer is the process through which we are to obtain things from God, this verse has special significance because believers are given the three different methods of how we are to obtain things that we need from God, which are through **"Asking, Seeking and Knocking."**

**"Ask"** implies a simple request or petition, in humility but with confidence, where believers ask for things that are consistent with His promise to give, that which will be best for you and that which will bring Him glory and praise.

**"Seek"** denotes application. It means to pursue after earnestly and to be diligent in your search. This does not mean **"every now and then"** you haphazardly look for when you are seeking. **No, it denotes a "passionate and on-going" quest at all costs. If you want to see the hand of God moving in your life then seek His face, for those that diligently seek Him shall find Him.** (Read Hebrews 11:6)

**"Knock"** shows endurance, persistence or perseverance despite any hindrances, obstacles, opposition or barriers of any kind.

While this verse indeed is a wonderful promise from our Lord, it is not to be considered as a **"blank check"** type of doctrine regarding prayer. The point here in this passage of scripture is not that God will randomly give us anything that we foolishly, lustfully, selfishly or sinfully want but **that we are to be diligent to ask in faith without doubting and to make full use of the means by which He grants blessings.**

Therefore, we are encouraged to always ask God for His help through prayer and not faint. **Remember that prayer doesn't make things easy, but it always makes things change.**

**THEREFORE, HAVE FAITH IN GOD!**

# 38

# "What Should You Do When Someone You Trusted Turns Against You?"

In this world filled with human depravity, no one is exempt from an attack rising from jealousy or envy. While it may begin with a silent whisper in a corner, then move to a closed door meeting and result in a full blown confrontation, those that walk upright with God are marked for an attack against them.

Such was the case in the life of Moses in Numbers Chapter 12, but more importantly, we are given the key principle on how we should handle these situations regardless if they occur in our home, place of business or even in our church.

Numbers 12: 1-2 NIV says, "Miriam and Aaron began to talk against Moses because of his Cushite wife, for he has married a Cushite. 'Has the LORD spoken only through Moses?' they asked. 'Hasn't he also spoken through us?' And the LORD heard this.

Miriam, as the sister of Moses, was a prophetess and held high rank among the women of Israel. As a young girl, she was the one who pushed baby Moses, in his sealed basket, down the Nile River until it was found by Pharaoh's daughter. She was the one who spoke up and recommended that Pharaoh's daughter get a nanny for the infant Moses and ran and got their very own mother. Later, upon the destruction of all the enemy at the Red Sea, she was the one that started singing and a great revival service broke out as Israel stood on the banks after God's miraculous deliverance.

But on this occasion, jealousy began to flood her heart as envy began to stir her soul. While all of the exact details are unrecorded in scripture, it's clearly evident that Miriam began to resent the wife of Moses, who was a descendant of Ham.

Perhaps Miriam believed Moses was indulging her too much, allowing himself to be swayed by her relationship, persuaded by her suggestions, and be led by her foreign feminine ways.. All of which she believed were effecting both her and Aaron's positions of authority and could diminish their reputations.

So, Miriam became the moving force or chief instigator in this attack against Moses, with Aaron allowing himself to be drawn into the opposition.

While they didn't deny Moses' prophetic leadership, they claimed equality with him as they began to dispute his judgment. Miriam reminded Israel that she was a prophetess and that Aaron also received divine revelations from God, being the high priest. In doing so, they glorified themselves as they tried to convince the people that Moses had no monopoly on God's communication and leadership towards Israel.

But our Lord, who reigns on high is a discerner of human hearts and will always have the final say-so in every matter. For as you read on throughout chapter 12, it was solely recorded to let all readers that "a person will always reap what they have sown." Even a God of grace is a God of judgment in the cases before Him.

Miriam was struck with leprosy and became "as white as snow." And the one she so vehemently spoke out against (Moses) had to intercede for her to be healed, cleansed, forgiven and restored.

How many pastors have returned from vacations only to discover that a once trusted minister on their staff has lured some members away? How many diligent employees have been affected by another back-stabbing, butt-kissing, and position stealing employee? How many people have faithfully performed in their role or assignment only to suffer loss because of another person's underhanded, manipulative, shady, corrupt and deceptive ways?

No matter how painful and hurtful these attacks may seem to be when they come, even if you suffer a loss, there's no room for your personal retaliation or revenge. Realize that your trusting Christ will always result in new doors or greater opportunities appearing.

And even if you never personally witness God's judgments on your attackers, they will answer to God and will also reap what they've sown and may have to come back before you to repent and ask for your prayers.

**THEREFORE, HAVE FAITH IN GOD!**

# 39

# "Does Your Life Exemplify Faith In Christ Or Are You the Only Person That Knows About it?

The bible stresses the importance of our life demonstrating faith towards God, other believers and even those outside the faith that you come in contact with. So having faith in Christ should not only have a profound effect on you, but should impact the lives surrounding you as you journey through life.

So the main question is: "Does your life exemplify faith in Christ or are you the only person who knows about it?"

In Romans 1:8, the Apostle Paul, in writing to the believers in Rome says, "I thank my God through Jesus Christ for you all, that your faith is spoken of throughout the whole world."

The Apostle Paul, in his salutation, begins to congratulate the believers in Rome for the notoriety of their faith.

During the new Testament times, Rome was the metropolis of the world. People came from all over to buy, sell, and trade their commerce, experience its wicked culture, participate in its immoral entertainment or to be involved in its corrupt political system with its earthly power.

A large church had been established in Rome long before Paul had arrived there. Many turned away from lives filled with idolatry, adultery, and corruption to walking in obedience in Christ, and now their faith was being celebrated by the apostle, even as he was imprisoned.

Their love for Jesus Christ and other believers, along with their testimonies towards unbelievers, their steadfastness in the face of persecution and their joy, even which Nero's threats of death couldn't quench, were spoken throughout the world.

They were thankful for their salvation and deliverance from sin and they rejoiced in God's wonderful grace that was being demonstrated towards them.

The main lesson for us today is that Paul commended those believers for their faith because faith is the basic virtue in the heart and life of a believer. For without it, you cannot please God,, all things are possible to him that believes. Do you have faith that God can see and is pleased with?

There are many today that testify or claim that they have faith or believe in God, but their actions and deeds clearly prove otherwise. Many just go to church to fulfil a routine obligation or to perform an outward ritual, but there's no life of faith.

Faith is not a mere possession or a trophy that you can just point to or sit on a shelf for its display. Faith is having a heart for God and the allowing Christ to reveal Himself through your life towards everything and everyone you come in contact with.

Faith is being led by the Holy Spirit and doing godly deeds despite all adverse circumstances or evil forces that may attempt to oppose or even persecute you.

Can Christ be seen in your life through deeds or the works you're doing? Is your life an example of the love of God? What works are you doing towards others that demonstrate the indwelling life of Jesus Christ?

A famous historian declared that the Roman Empire fell, not because of the rise of another attacking foreign power, but due to the preaching of the Gospel and the love of Christ that was exemplified through the lives of the believers.

You too should be impacting and influencing your world for Christ, for in doing so, others will clearly see God touching lives through the love of Jesus Christ.

**THEREFORE, HAVE FAITH IN GOD!**

# 40

# "I Thought You Said You Were Going To Serve Me?"

These were the loving words that The Holy Spirit spoke to a dear lady that I was ministering to a few days ago. The Lord was reminding her of His love towards her as she was wrestling with her commitment and full surrender.

Have you made a vow or commitment to the Lord and you're failing to keep it? So often people "Flirt" around with the different aspects of sin or the world until their passion for Christ begins to diminish and grow cold.

While we struggle in dealing with the cares of the world, the love of the flesh is often the cause of many turning back from Biblical truths and the fellowship of Jesus Christ.

In II Timothy 4:10, the Apostle Paul referring to one of his co-workers said, "For Demas hath forsaken me, having loved this present world, and is departed unto Thessalonica…"

Demas, who was a Gentile convert and became a close laborer with the apostle, could no longer bear the suffering that was going on with preaching the Gospel with Paul. This once faithful companion of Paul, who had been with him during the first imprisonment of the Apostle at Rome, now began to allow his heart to turn away.

The Holy Spirit of God will always commune with your heart as a believer begins to gradually move in the wrong direction.

Nevertheless, Demas still allowed his heart to turn away and deserted from the ministry he had been called to do.

He lacked the courage to stand, then permitted himself to succumb to the enticement or temptation of the things that he misses and chose to abdicate his faith and abandon the work.

This was not a decision he made at the spur of the moment. Despite the grace of God and the communion of the Holy spirit, a person gradually allows the devil to speak to their mind, challenge their thinking, entertain their conscious and then shipwreck their faith in God.

Demas was not some sort of monster, but like so many, he failed to resist the constant attractions or seductions and returned to the sins of thee past. Whether it was lust of the flesh, or desired wealth, or the comfort away from the persecutions of ministry, he turned his back on his Savior and the friendship, honor and duty of serving God with the Apostle Paul.

Don't become a "Demas" and run away. When we are weak, know that He is strong and we can be led and made to stand in the power of His might. Know that there is nothing that you cannot overcome in this world through Jesus Christ.

Once you've accepted Christ and have become a "partaker of His Divine nature by being filled with His Spirit," YOU ARE NEVER ALONE!

Run to Him, not away from him. Draw closer to Him and listen to His voice. Allow the Holy spirit to direct your path and experience the wonderful joy of walking with Jesus Christ.

# About The Author

*MISTAKES!!!* Life doesn't come without having made some, and I've made my share of them which have greatly affected my life.

### *But by the Grace of God, they didn't cost my life.*

Now it's out of both my learned experiences and my fellowship with The Lord, as I firmly stand on God's Word in faith, that I preach and offer these inspired and prophetic messages of Salvation, Grace, Deliverance, Healing, Power, **and Victory through Jesus Christ.**

Since I've faced some of the most **"incredible impossibilities"** a person could ever face, my purpose is to help you understand God's Love, Mercy, Forgiveness, Strength and Power in the face of adverse circumstances, negative situations, painful conditions, and satanic entrapments that threaten your life, home, and family.

### *You Too Can Be Victorious Through Faith In Jesus Christ!*

While **Andrew Bills** is a loving husband, father and grandfather, he has preached in various churches including Baptists, Pentecostal, Charismatic Catholic, and Non-Denominational Faith Ministries, despite any minor doctrinal differences, he continues to reach out and touch lives in today's world with the very inspiring and special message of **"Victory Thru Calvary."**

He's been in ministry for over 30 years, has a Bachelor's Degree and has served in many different capacities including Pastor, Lecturer, Advisor, Broadcaster, Author, Evangelist and in various managerial positions throughout the Logistics & Warehousing Industry.

As a preacher of Jesus Christ and as a teacher to the Body of Christ, he's influenced many as he continues to build Faith, brings Hope, Joy, Inspiration, and Deliverance to many hungry souls.

# Books By Andrew Bills

Increase your library with these life-changing, scriptural, practical, powerful and victorious readable books of faith and wisdom from The Holy Spirit of God.

*Up From The Ashes*

*There's No Such Thing As A Hopeless Situation*

*Never Step Down To The Level Of Your Circumstances*

*How Long Should You Wait For Your Prayers To Be Answered?*

*How To Stop The Devil From Squeezing The Life Out Of You*

*Will You Trust Me Even If You Don't Understand
Or Can't See What I'm Doing?*

*Having Faith That God Can See*

*How To Overcome Your Wounded Past*

# Ministry Contact Information:

### Andrew Bills Ministries Inc.

*"The Victory Report Hour"*

**PO Box 6811,   Orange, CA  92863**

Website Address:

**www.andrewbills.com**

Email Address:

**andrewbillsministries@yahoo.com**

24013736R00081

Made in the USA
San Bernardino, CA
10 September 2015